My family has walked the floors ... held the babies of Harmony Outr... ...mil-ily, love them, and love Christ more because of them. I think you will as well.

—MAX LUCADO, Senior Minister, Oak Hills Church, San Antonio, and a *New York Times* best-selling author

The first time I heard Lisa tell Levi's story, I had an unsettling thought: Lisa Bentley knows God in ways I don't know Him yet. Her tender, obedient response to God's call of compassion made me hungry to know Him like she does. While I'm not sure how many other "Lisas" there are in our self-centered world, I'm positive that there are millions of other "Levis"—children left to live alone and perhaps die alone. Lisa stands as a humble example of what can happen when a man or woman actually lives out the truth that God cares for orphans.

—KAY WARREN, Saddleback Church, San Clemente, California

I salute John and Lisa Bentley for their tireless devotion to serving those in need. Their efforts have had a profound impact in terms of touching and brightening the lives of countless children. By reaching out and providing love and medical care to each child at Harmony Outreach, the Bentleys are showing to the rest of the world the tremendous good that can come from exporting America's compassion and generosity.

—TOMMY THOMPSON, former Secretary of Health and
Human Services and Governor of Wisconsin

Everyone should hear Levi's story! I've been privileged to watch this miraculous story unfold over the last few years. Hearing the God-sized details of how Levi's life was saved and seeing God's people come together for the cause of this little boy serve as an inspiration to us all.

—MARY BETH CHAPMAN, Cofounder, Shaohannah's
Hope Foundation, Lansdowne, Virginia

Saving Levi

Left to Die . . .
Destined to Live

FOCUS ON THE FAMILY®

Saving Levi

Left to Die . . .
Destined to Live

by

Lisa Misraje Bentley

 Tyndale House Publishers, Inc., Carol Stream, Illinois

Editor: Marianne Hering
Cover design: Tracy Watkins
Cover photo and photo on page iv by: David G. McIntyre–Black Star
Cover copy by: Carol Hubbard

Printed in the United States of America
1 2 3 4 5 6 7 8 9 / 12 11 10 09 08 07

ISBN 10: 1-58997-449-2
ISBN 13: 978-1-58997-449-4

To John,
my husband, my love, and my best friend

and

To Emily, Ian, Orly, Oliver, Donald "Reid," and Levi,
my children, my treasure, and my joy

because He lives.

Contents

Acknowledgments

As always, this book was made possible by the love, encouragement, and support of all my friends and family. Although you are too numerous to name, I hope you know who you are and what role you played in my life.

I am very grateful to my agent, Bucky Rosenbaum, for his support throughout this project. Bucky, thank you also for the eloquent way that you handle people and for your tremendous insight and wise counsel. (You rock!)

Nanci McAlister, my product manager—1,000 flowers off to you! Nanci, you held us all together throughout the grueling publishing process of a fast-track book, and from two different time zones and countries. I owe you big time! I will miss your "go to bed" e-mails.

Marian Liautaud—Wow Mar, where do I start? Thank you for leaving your family and traveling to China to capture my story and take in the sights and sounds of China. I am so very grateful for your talent and expertise in helping me put Levi's story into print. Thanks for making me look smarter than I am.

Marianne Hering, my editor—You took what we gave you and made it the best it could be. You filled in the cracks, buffed, and polished this work until it shined.

And much thanks to John, my husband—You came in at the 11th hour and helped with the rewrites. All my love and sincere thanks. Oh yeah, and thank you for bringing me to China!

My six precious children (Emily, Ian, Orly, Oliver, Donald "Reid," and Levi), all of whom I love to spend my time with. You are so much fun. I love you dearly. You are my treasure. Go team Bentley!

Allen Tappe—Thank you, Allen, for your unwavering belief in my worth. I love you!

My mom, Donna Misraje, who raised us three kids as a single mom—I love you more!

My dad, Donald Misraje (still "Daddy" to me)—You are the best dad. God broke the mold when He made you. I love you!

Carol Misraje, my step mom—Thank you for being part of my life. I love you!

To my Texas Cowboys/Cowgirls who loved on us and let us be ourselves while living on your beautiful soil: Rick Atchley, James Bankes, Larry and Susan Buck, Andre and Camilla Carter, Diane Carroll, Lonnie Diggs, Bill and Barbara New, Gary Smith, and Barbara Tappe.

To my cousin Susie Schmitt, a writer, who convinced me that this book needed to be written. Thanks for your great advice during this whole process. Thanks also for traveling to Kaifeng with me!!

And a huge kiss to my favorite artist, G. Harvey, and Patti Jones (John's uncle and aunt), for introducing us to the great folks at Focus on the Family. John and I get a glimpse of Jesus through your humility and kindness toward us and so many others.

Max Lucado—Oliver and Orly would like me to apologize for their hitting you in the head with an empty water bottle while you were in China. They told me, "We just wanted his attention."

Tyndale Publishing House—Thank you for allowing me the opportunity to tell my story. I hope we hit one out of the ball field!

David McIntyre of Black Star Photo Agency (a true L.A. guy)—You were my first choice and I am so thankful you were able to squeeze us in.

I want to thank all the hard-working staff at our orphanage, "Harmony Outreach." Thank you for taking such good care of our precious orphans while I have been busy writing this book.

I have many Chinese people and organizations to thank. Here are just a few: Mr. Wang, who picked up Levi in the field, Langfang Petroleum Pipeline Hospital, Langfang City Hospital, Children's Hope International, China Center for Adoption Affairs, Civil Affairs Ministry, China Charity Federation, Beijing Children's Hospital and Dr. Chee, Hebei Provincial Police Department, Director Yan of the Langfang Orphanage. We also want to thank Mark Wei and Lily Huang, and our nanny Xiao Gi who has helped us care for Levi since he first returned to China.

I would like to thank the following for holding up our hands along the way: United Airlines, Ed and Carol Wong, Holiday Inn Select of Boston, Robarts Interiors, Life Outreach International, Shriners Hospitals for Children of Boston and Northern California, the Texas Scottish Rites Hospital–Dallas, Dr. Greg Tobin, my Beijing Beth Moore Bible teacher and gal pal, Doreen Yata, Kehillat Beijing. Tim and Pam Baker—Thanks for the ride! My Chinese sister Melody Zhang and her boss Dwyatt Gantt of Children's Hope International—Thank you for having the heart and eyes of Jesus. My good friend Patti Coffey at the Anthony Robbins Foundation—Thank you for being an honest and loyal coach.

Steven and Mary Beth Chapman—Thank you for your friendship and for seeing us through both Orly and Levi's adoptions.

Special thanks to the incredible talent of Tony B. Design, who created the Harmony Outreach logo and to Kay Warren for being a godly inspiration and for all you are doing for people with AIDS.

In memory of my dear friend Pam Kolva, who went home to be with the Lord during the writing of this book. Thank you for encouraging me and loving my family. Your leaving really came unexpectedly. We miss you, Aunt Pammy!

While writing this book I was inspired by the following musicians: Mary J. Blige (MJB) rock on!, Johnny Cash, Bono, Cyndi Lauper, Eva Cassidy, Jack Johnson, Derek Webb, Sara Groves, and Rich Mullins.

Thanks to special places: The Orchard restaurant in Beijing (nicest restaurant in Beijing, and off the beaten path), the Holiday Inn Lido Starbucks (where all the magic happens), The Book Worm (great internet/cafe/hangout), and the freeway where I listen to my music.

Thank you for taking the time to read this book.

"Watch, Smile, Dance."

Tender blessings,

Lisa

Prologue

I WEAR A MEDALLION OF THE ancient Chinese *shu* character around my neck. A Jewish girlfriend gave it to me to symbolize the work God has given me to do. Ironically, this character no longer exists, but for me it remains significant. It represents the concept of not only seeing your brother's pain, but also feeling it. It reminds me of the Good Samaritan.

    —Tender blessings as you read Levi's story,
       Lisa

I will not die. I will live.

—PSALM 118:17 (NIRV)

CHAPTER ONE

Left to Die

"The kingdom of heaven is like
treasure hidden in a field."
—Matthew 13:44

It would be 24 hours from the time Levi was left to die in the field until I first saw him.

That March, like all Marches, came damp and dreary to Northern China. That morning was no exception. As another gray day awakened, a baby's cries pierced the drizzly dawn in a village on the outskirts of the city of Langfang.

One by one, villagers heard the wail, a sound like a wounded animal begging to be put out of its misery. But it wasn't a cat or a fox. Drawn toward the persistent, shrill cries, a peasant farmer wandered farther into the fallow cornfield where he found a baby.

Word spread that a child had been abandoned in a nearby field. Within the hour at least 40 villagers came to see. All of them stared in shock as they encircled the baby.

Before them lay an infant, no more than six weeks old, crying in agony. He was wrapped in crimson silk and dressed in a once-beautiful, bright yellow outfit—now soaked through with body fluids and blood. This baby's face had been severely burned; he didn't have long to live.

Aghast at the baby's condition, the villagers stood paralyzed, unable to respond. Should they pick him up? Should they take him to the hospital? Who was willing to take on this burden? What future would this child possibly have?

Child abandonment in China is a double-edged sword. Because of their child's critical burns, this baby's parents probably felt they had no choice but to leave him in a field where he would either die peacefully or be rescued. And yet if they were caught abandoning their baby, they would receive a strict punishment—a heavy fine and possible prison time. Already poor, they would never be able to pay the financial price. And jail time would mean losing the means to support the rest of their family. Instead, they would live the rest of their days with the memory of abandoning their baby.

The villagers knew there could be a price to pay for getting involved. They knew they would have to answer the authorities' questions: Why do you have this child in your possession? Who was responsible for his injuries? Who are the parents? Are you protecting them? How will you pay for his medical treatment?

No one in this poor little village had money to help. They had families of their own—too many mouths to feed already. What point would there be in taking in one more, especially one who looked ready to cross the threshold of death's door? Who was willing to risk complicating his life for that of a severely burned infant? After all, he probably wouldn't live until morning anyway.

For two full hours, the ring of villagers remained, talking in hushed voices about what to do, scrutinizing with curiosity the infant's burns. Gradually, the villagers began to shuffle away. Though they felt sad for the infant, his case seemed futile. What good would it do to help this dying baby?

The sky had lightened, signaling time for the village farmers to head to work. The baby's cries continued, disturbing the morning and the memories of those who had just seen him.

One by one, the villagers had left. All except for one man—Mr. Wang. Fiftyish, dark-skinned, and taller than most Chinese men, he shifted from foot to foot, wondering what he should do. There lay a baby, cold, afraid, and in excruciating pain. Mr. Wang took pity on him. With grown children of his own and a young grandchild living in his home, he could not bring himself to leave the child to die. As if begging for Mr. Wang to make a decision, the baby's shrieks took on a more desperate pitch in the desolation of the field.

Alone now, Mr. Wang moved close enough to notice that the baby's head had been shaved and a bandage still remained where an IV had been inserted. Someone had already brought this baby to a village clinic. In China, they often give babies medicine through an IV in the scalp. The baby's parents probably brought him to the farm doctor after the terrible accident. Mr. Wang tried to imagine what might have happened the night before. Maybe the electricity had gone out again, like it often does in the villages. Maybe the family had been working outside and placed a candle too close to the crib. Perhaps it fell over and started the bedding on fire. When the parents brought him to the farm doctor, he probably said, "Save what little money you have. This child will die soon."

Mr. Wang could only imagine the pain this baby's parents must have felt when faced with the excruciating decision to let their son go. With children of his own, he couldn't envision having to wrap a child in burial clothes and leave him in a field to die.

I can save this baby. I will raise him as my own child.

Before he realized what he was doing, Mr. Wang stooped down and gently scooped the baby from the ground. He rocked the baby back and forth, pressing him against his chest so that he could hear his heartbeat. The rhythmic sound of compassion stilled the infant, now quiet for the first time that morning.

What now? What do I do with this dying baby? Filled with resolve and fear at the same time, he mounted his bicycle and, with one hand on the bar and one arm supporting the baby, he pedaled as quickly as he could to his home where his wife would be waiting to hear what all the stir was about in the field. *How will I explain all of this to her? What will she say when I show her the baby?*

When Mr. Wang reached his cement-block house, he came to a smooth stop, being careful not to jostle the baby. He gingerly swung his leg around and dismounted the bike, putting as little pressure against the baby's body as possible. Hesitantly, he approached the front door. "What happened?" his wife asked. Suddenly, she noticed the bundle he was holding.

"Let's go inside," he said. Gently, he laid the baby on the only bed in their one room, cement-floor house.

"Oh, no!" she gasped. Her hands flew up to cover her mouth, and horror blanketed her face. Mr. Wang tried to explain how and where he had discovered the child, but the baby's sudden wails made it impossible to talk. While he rocked the baby, his wife searched frantically for a bottle. Finding neither a bottle nor milk, Mr. Wang placed the baby in his wife's arms and pedaled off on his well-worn bike to the village store, which was just minutes from their house and tucked down an alleyway. This store was a shack where the locals bought essential items like tea and powdered baby milk. Mr. Wang quickly paid for these items and sped back home.

The baby was screaming full force by now. Nothing Mrs. Wang did would calm him. Quickly, Mr. Wang mixed the powdered formula with water. At the first sip of milk, relief washed over the baby. He sucked the bottle dry in what seemed like one giant slurp. Mr. Wang quickly mixed another bottle, and again the baby emptied the bottle in seconds.

Satisfied from the warm milk, the baby quieted down enough for Mr. Wang to lay him out on the bed again. As delicately as he could, he pulled back the outer crimson blanket. Next, he carefully began opening up the yellow silk burial outfit, which was now sticking to his skin from the blood and body fluids that continued to seep from his wounds. When he opened the infant's clothes to examine the burns, he recoiled, nearly stumbling backward into the little table in the middle of the room. This was not a baby. Mr. Wang had never seen anything like it. The baby's face was burned along his jaw line, his skin melted from one ear down around the chin to the other ear, including the areas around his mouth. His entire left side was seared, leaving the muscles and tissue along his torso exposed. Flames had singed away all of the skin from his left shoulder down to his hip. His left arm was so charred that when he tried to lift it up, ashes fell from it. His little hand had already turned black, as had his knee.

Inside the baby's blanket, Mr. Wang discovered ten RMB (or renminbi, the equivalent of approximately U.S.$1.25). The parents must have spent all they could afford with the farm doctor, tucking what was left over into his blanket to pay for his passage into the next life.

But he's not dead! Mr. Wang wanted to shout. *Did the parents know someone would find him in that field? What were they expecting? How can I help this dying baby?*

Seeing the severity of the baby's open wounds, Mr. Wang realized immediately he would not be able to simply love this baby back to health. In fact, with each minute that passed, the child's wounds worsened and his strength ebbed.

Desperate for help, Mr. Wang, again cradling the baby in one arm, biked down to the village leader's house. It was still early in the morning as Mr. Wang explained how he had found the baby. Then he begged the leader, "Can you help him?"

Stunned at the state of the child swaddled against Mr. Wang's chest, the leader struggled to find words. Shaking his head in hopelessness, he said, "There is nothing I can do to help this baby." Seeing Mr. Wang's despair, he tried to offer a rational perspective: "If a horse breaks a leg, we would put it out of its misery. In this baby's grave condition, we probably need to take the same view and let nature take its course."

Mr. Wang refused to accept this. He got back on his bicycle, now in a race against time. He had only one option left.

Undeterred by the village leader's inability to help the baby, Mr. Wang pedaled several miles to the Langfang Civil Affairs Ministry. Knowing this government agency would find the baby within the hour, he wrapped the infant in his crimson blanket and gingerly placed him on the front steps of the newly constructed glass and cement ministry building. The stark contrast between the baby's disfigured appearance and the polished facade of the building highlighted the disparity of life in China. On the one hand, Langfang, the larger city surrounding Mr. Wang's village, was bustling with development. Cranes perched atop the roofs of newly erected high-rise buildings. And yet, even in the midst of all this modernization, Mr. Wang still rode his bicycle to work every day, like hundreds of others. Too poor to afford a car, he pedaled back and forth to the fields where he labored each day.

Today, though, was not an ordinary workday. This would be a day he would never forget. Gently patting the crying infant, Mr. Wang tried to reassure him before saying good-bye. *Is this how his parents felt before they left him?* Mr. Wang knew he was this child's only friend, and now he, too, would be abandoning him. With fear and sadness, he mounted his bicycle. As he began riding away, he took one last look at the baby lying alone on the cement steps. Pedaling as if he were trying to ride away from a nightmare, he breathed the only prayer left, "Please, save him."

My family had been in China only a few weeks when we heard about this severely injured child. We had come to China to work at a small and struggling orphanage in Langfang. The city of Langfang is a perfect microcosm of the evolution taking place in China. Over half a million people live in this city, which is undergoing incredible expansion. Basic infrastructure improvements are being made on a large scale.

Like an expectant host getting ready to throw a big party, Langfang is constantly abuzz with preparations. Construction projects dot the city. Their new, expansive four-lane boulevards divided by ornate flower gardens and larger-than-life outdoor sculptures make you feel as if you might have arrived at the party too soon, though. While there's a lot of hustle and bustle, the dichotomy between sharing traffic lanes with cars, bikes, rigged-up motor scooters with two or three passengers, and shepherds and their bleating flocks of sheep makes the perfectly paved roads seem, well, like too much, too soon. It's as if China is way in front of the growth curve in some ways, and yet preposterously behind the times in others.

On these same magnificent new thoroughfares, for instance, they still hire elderly peasants to sweep the streets—by hand with brooms made of horsehair or stiff, leafy bristles of some kind. And the gardens are planted and maintained by peasant farmers who ride their bikes to whatever plot they've been assigned to that day and park them in the middle of the road.

This same dichotomy of the ancient struggling to become modern existed in the home we were renting. My husband, John, had picked out a house for us to rent before I arrived in China with the kids. He had told me how wonderful it was. It was near the home of our orphanage teammates, Tim and Pam Baker. The picture he had painted and the reality of the house were quite different. On the outside, with its cement block styling and contemporary lines, it looked somewhat twenty-first century. And yet inside, we had no heat. Having arrived in November, we had to wear two layers of clothing at all times. For all of its modern design, none of the toilets had been updated. No matter how hard I tried, I just could not get used to the squat pot toilets—holes cut in the floor where you simply crouch down, take aim, and hope for the best.

The rats, which made their presence known by scampering up and down the inside of the walls, were taking their toll on all of us. I suppose I should have been grateful they stayed on the inside and didn't venture out where we could see them. But hearing them jumping around inside the walls and multiplying day by day put all of us on edge.

Within only one hour of moving into that house, I knew I wanted to move out. However, we liked the neighborhood where we lived. It was a gated community with about 100 homes, which we had dubbed the Langfang Children's Village. This is where the first two foster homes had been opened, and more were in the works. Unfortunately, one man owned most of the homes in the neighborhood, so few were available to purchase. After almost giving up hope, we were thankful to stumble onto one that was available. It was spacious and more westernized—the toilets were above ground. A little garden decorated the backyard, making it feel homier. We had put an offer on the home earlier that day, which the Canadian owners accepted. We were elated at the prospect of moving out of the heatless house of multiplying rats. We had gone over to Tim and Pam's to celebrate and had just sat down to watch an action movie when the phone rang.

Tim answered it in the next room, and I overheard him talking to Mark Wei. Mark was Tim's right-hand man. They had met each other while working together for the Christian Broadcasting Network (CBN) in China. When Tim decided to leave his post as director of CBN China to pursue full-time orphan-relief work, Mark followed him. As a Chinese national, Mark knows the ins and outs of dealing with government agencies and is adept at forging warm relationships with people in key positions throughout China. Although Mark is a man of few words, he is a hard worker. Despite our blue-jeans-and T-shirt dress code at work, Mark always dressed in slacks, a shirt and tie, and dress shoes—ready to put in a serious day of work.

Mark speaks excellent English and understands the nuances of Chinese culture. When we would make mistakes in our interactions with the Chinese, Mark would make everything right again. Mark and John became friends quickly and worked side by side to develop relationships throughout China, which, on this particular night, would prove to be life saving.

"Mr. Yan says the Langfang Orphanage has a severely burned baby," Mark told Tim. "Someone from the Langfang Civil Affairs Ministry found him on the front steps this morning. The baby doesn't look like he'll make it. Do you think we can try to help?"

"Yes, of course we will help," Tim responded. "We'll be right over to pick up the baby." Mark had been key in establishing a relationship with Mr. Yan, the director of the Langfang Orphanage, whom we had met earlier when we took in two at-risk babies. Mr. Yan knew he could count on us to give his special-needs babies the help they required. John and Tim began putting on their coats for the journey to the Langfang Orphanage. Before the two could make it out the door, the phone rang a second time.

It was Mr. Yan calling to say that the police had just found another abandoned newborn who was missing three fingers and appeared to have pneumonia. "Could we also take him?" Mark asked Tim. Tim agreed to take in both babies, and he, John, and Ann Lo, another orphanage staffer who had been babysitting our children, quickly headed out the door into the drizzly darkness.

The Langfang Orphanage was a 20-minute drive. Continuing just beyond the McDonald's on the main boulevard, they turned into an alleyway and parked the van outside the entrance of the orphanage.

The Langfang Orphanage was severely underresourced, and Mr. Yan greeted them at the door. When he ushered John and Tim into the crude concrete structure, they were struck by the smell of vomit. The dirty, white-washed walls and dilapidated furniture and light fixtures underscored the dejection of the setting. With nearly 20 orphans in his care and only a few nannies to support them, Mr. Yan simply could not provide the attention these children needed. As for the other orphans they saw, there were several mentally challenged older children who all looked dirty. Between the vomit and the unkempt, handicapped children, an air of hopelessness permeated the place. Seeing the burned child for the first time only reinforced the despair.

When Mr. Yan left the room to get the infant, they weren't sure what to expect. John and Tim had cared for children with all kinds of medical problems. But when they saw this baby, they were shocked. Their experience had not prepared them for the disfigurement that confronted them.

The foul smell of body fluids came from the child's burned limbs. Even though the Wangs had cleaned up his yellow outfit and blanket, it was completely soaked through again. *How did this child get so badly burned?* they wondered. Amazed that an infant could survive such critical injuries, Tim scooped up the fragile baby and considered what they could do to save him.

While Tim tried to soothe the baby who was now crying in pain, Mr. Yan handed the newborn with pneumonia over to

John. As quickly as they could, they packed the two babies into the car and drove away. The smell of burned flesh filled the car and the men's hearts with a tangible, painful urgency.

They arrived at the dimly lit Langfang Petroleum Pipeline Hospital at eight o'clock that night. John and Tim rushed through the doors of the pediatric wing, their senses greeted by the stench of stale urine, the sight of dilapidated rooms, peeling paint, half-finished construction projects, and children crying in the hallways. Mark Wei and Ann Lo had driven separately and met John and Tim at the hospital.

Nurses quickly approached the foursome to see what they were doing there. When they peeked into the bloody blanket, shock registered on each face. The baby's hands were black like charcoal. With no pain reliever to diminish his agony, he was feeling the full intensity of his burns; even in his weakened state, the baby's wails filled the room.

The nurses ushered John and the three others into an examining room in the hospital's burn unit. The walls were two-tone, the bottom half painted in green to represent serenity, the upper half off-white. Instead of creating a serene setting, the peeling green paint simply served to symbolize the sickly state of this dying baby. With a sense of urgency, the nurse performed a quick assessment of his vital signs. Crowded into the room, the group waited for a doctor to arrive. John, who had the responsibility to write the organization's monthly newsletters, pulled out his digital camera to capture the moment. John knew we would have an amazing story to tell.

A tall doctor in his mid-40s and wearing a white lab coat

appeared minutes later. In dry, unemotional terms he spelled out in Chinese the child's chances for survival: "I've seen a lot of burn victims, but I've never treated an infant this badly burned," he said. "At best, this baby has a 20 percent chance of surviving." Mark translated the ominous prognosis.

"I don't care what it takes," Tim told the doctor. "Spare no expense. We will not give up on this baby."

Though he did not hold out much hope for the child, the doctor respected our team's desire to save him. He knew they were relying on him to fight for the baby and do whatever he could.

The doctor instructed the nurses to gently remove the baby's clothes. Fluids had seeped out and soaked his garments, causing the fabric to stick to his open wounds. With painstaking care, the nurse cut away his clothes and proceeded to scrub the burned flesh from his body. Although this is an intensely painful procedure, they had to do it to ensure the wounds were not infected. The child thrashed and fought against the cleaning process. Thankfully, step two was much easier and offered him his first real relief from the burning. The doctor dipped what looked like a paint brush into a white, creamy ointment that resembled milk of magnesia. He lightly stroked the infant's burns with the salve, finally providing some cooling relief to his skin. For nearly three days he had endured the full magnitude of pain with no relief from his third-degree burns.

Having completed the first round of rescue measures for the baby, the nurse delicately diapered him and took him to the intensive care unit where she placed him in an incubator. The nurses seemed to be providing special attention for him.

"The baby's chances of living are extremely poor," the doctor warned John, Tim, Mark, and Ann before they left. "Even if he survives, we will still have to amputate most of his limbs." After announcing this grim prognosis, he added as an afterthought, "Let me take your cell phone number. I'll call you when the baby has died."

John and Tim returned home late that night, the smell of body fluids lingering on their clothes. Pam washed Tim's shirt and pants several times before they finally came clean.

When John got home, he told me everything that had happened at the hospital. I slept restlessly through the night, and when I awoke the next morning, I called Ann Lo and asked, "Will you come with me to the hospital to see the new burned baby?"

I had no idea how this simple decision would change my life.

CHAPTER TWO

China Heart

To the world you might be just one person,
but to one person, you just might be the world.
—AUTHOR UNKNOWN

救

I CAME TO CHINA DRAGGING my feet. In fact, I really had no interest in coming to China at all—except for the growing restlessness I was feeling inside. John had a good job as a lawyer in the Pacific Northwest, and we were living the American dream—four kids, a minivan in the driveway, sports car in the garage, and a brand-new four-bedroom house. It was everything we'd hoped for. And yet, one day I prayed, "God, if this is all there is to life, then this is boring and it stinks."

I guess I was looking for a change. But never in my wildest imagination did I think God would send me to China as the solution to my discontent. How could moving somewhere ten thousand miles away, to a place where I don't speak the language or understand anything about the culture, be His best for me?

My husband, John, had always wanted to work with Chinese orphans. He lured me to China by telling me we would go only for an extended visit. On this three-month tour I would home-school the kids and check it out. The deal was, if after three months I didn't feel called to China, I could veto it and he would bring us back to the States where he would resume practicing law.

Initially, we went to China to work with Tim and Pam Baker. They were trying to launch an orphanage for special-needs children under the Philip Hayden Foundation. Philip Hayden had been one of Tim's closest friends from the time Tim and Pam first moved to China 10 years earlier. Tim worked with Phil at University Language Services where they oversaw an English language program throughout China. Together, they traveled the provinces to visit the schools that offered the language program. Tim and Phil shared a passion for orphan-relief work. As they traveled for work, they also made it a point to visit local orphanages to see what they could do to help. On one of their train trips across the countryside, Philip, age 23, suffered a massive heart attack and died instantly. His autopsy revealed that he had the rare heart condition called Marfan's syndrome. Tim wanted to carry on Phil's legacy by starting a foundation named after his friend.

One month into our visit I still felt pretty cold to the whole China experiment. Of course I felt for the orphans, I loved being able to help them, and our life definitely was not boring anymore. But I just didn't have a heart for the Chinese people.

That was before I saw the burned baby.

救

I had asked Ann Lo to accompany me back to the hospital where she had met up with John, Tim, and Mark the night before. I was the only foreign woman on our team who had a driver's license. Driving in China is no small feat. Many times it feels as if you are on Mr. Toad's Wild Ride—without the safety features. There's a saying I learned right after arriving in China: The Chinese would rather die tragically than live tamely. This thinking is best reflected in their driving. If you die in China, there's a good chance it will be in a car accident. I know that sounds morbid, but the Chinese drive like maniacs. It's as if there are no rules of the road. Horrific car wrecks are a daily site along the highway. Even though I love the freedom of being able to jump in my van and listen to the radio while I drive around town, I live in constant fear of being killed behind the wheel. Our micro-minivan or "mian di" was shaped like a loaf of Wonder Bread and felt like it was made of tin. I asked God for protection as I set out for Ann Lo's house and cautiously made my way through traffic. I tried to imagine what I would encounter when we arrived at the hospital. John warned me that it was pretty bad. My heart hurt just picturing the agony this little boy must be in, and with no one to soothe and comfort him.

A low-rise brick building, the hospital looked fairly westernized on the outside. Inside, however, things were neither modern nor antiseptic. The examining rooms were small and dingy. Ann led the way toward the intensive care unit, which was closed off in an attempt to keep people and germs at bay. I noticed nurses peering through the glass dividing wall, checking to see how the burned baby was doing. After Ann identified herself to the nurse, they let us into his room where he lay alone in an incubator. The room was unnaturally quiet. He lay motionless, eyes closed, covered in white lotion, presumably to cool the burning sensation over his entire body.

Forsaken. That was all I could think. How could someone so helpless be left alone in his pain with no mother to hold him? It broke my heart to see him lying there. This baby was experiencing the loneliest hours any human being could endure. This infant had been abandoned by the people who should have protected him. No one was there to stay with him through the long watches of the night. Just then the baby's eyes flickered. In a flash, his eyes opened and he looked right at me, expectantly, as if to say, "Are you my mother?"

I knew right then that I would never look back at the life I had left behind.

救

You might think it natural that I fell in love with this distressed little baby. Only a person with a heart of stone would be able to look upon his pain and not feel compassion. But what you don't know about me is that I had an irrational fear that everything in life was conspiring to kill me, or worse, my kids. I operated like a character trapped in a Woody Allen movie, neurotically imagining everything is out to get me. One of the biggest reasons I didn't want to come to China in the first place was because I was so afraid we'd all die. This fear was born in me even before Severe Acute Respiratory Syndrome, better known as SARS, was on the radar, which would have given me a justifiable reason not to go to China. In the United States, food safety classes are required before restaurateurs can hang their "open" sign, and sanitary gloves are worn (and changed) with every patient in a hospital.

But here lay a baby, naked and covered only in white ointment, and all I could think was, *Who will stand in the gap for this baby?*

I knelt next to the incubator and examined little Wang Danli, or Daniel, as he had now been named. The poor little guy was trying desperately to suck his thumb, but it had been so badly burned. Every time he tried putting it into his mouth, he cried out in pain. He desperately needed some way to comfort himself. *I can't take this any more. If this were my child, I would do anything to save him.* In that moment, I knew what I needed to do. I called Tim.

When Tim answered the phone, his voice sounded groggy from being up late the night before. "Hi, Tim. I want to ask you two favors," I said. "First, I'd like to know if I could change the two babies' names from Daniel and Job to Levi and Asher."

"Come on, Lisa," he replied. "I just sent out a mass e-mail to supporters around the world to pray for baby *Danli*. Plus, all of the paperwork has been filed registering him with the government as Danli. It'll take too much work to change it."

"Tim, I feel strongly about this," I said. I didn't know what the name meant, but I always thought it had a neat sound. "Also, I'd like to take the lead on helping to save Levi." I continued. "Someone needs to be advocating for this baby and making sure he gets the best of the best care possible. I'd like to be that person."

Tim sensed the conviction in my voice. Even though changing the baby's name would be a hassle, he agreed to do it.

This baby had stolen my heart. Surprisingly, in return, he gave me my China heart.

CHAPTER THREE

Fire Gift

We are not human people having a spiritual experience;
we are spiritual people having a human experience.
—SUSAN SAINT JAMES ON *THE OPRAH WINFREY SHOW*

I STOOD WATCH BY LEVI'S incubator while nurses purposefully moved in and out of the ICU, monitoring his condition and continually replacing his IV fluid drip bags. My mind was trying to process the reality of what lay before me: a baby suffering third-degree burns over most of his body, with wounds so deep in some spots I could actually see muscle and bone. For every degree Levi's skin had been seared, compassion for this child flamed more deeply in my heart. *What now?* I didn't walk into this room expecting my heart to spontaneously combust. And yet I knew from that moment on, I would never be able to extinguish the fire that burned in me. No matter what it took, I was determined to save this child and give him a good life.

The next day I returned to the hospital to see Levi again, this time with our daughter, Emily. "Mom, can I go with you to the hospital tomorrow to see the baby?" Emily had asked. At eight years old, she displayed an uncommon compassion for hurting children, like the ones in the orphanage where we worked. I tried to prepare her for the graphic scene she was about to see, but really, there was no way to soften the blow: Levi's burns were severe. Emily gasped under her breath when she first saw him. With blackened, ashen limbs and an ointment-covered face, there was little about Levi that resembled a baby. Writhing in pain in his incubator, it appeared he had had a fitful night. Just as this scene had inflamed me the day before, seeing Levi was like having a wick lighted directly to Emily's heart. Within minutes she was aflame with love and compassion for him. Her nose nearly pressed against the incubator glass, Emily cooed to Levi like a mother dove to her chick. Seeing my daughter respond as I had the day before, I realized the risk we were taking: All of us were in danger of having our hearts broken.

It was a risk we were willing to take.

Minutes later, doctors came in the room to give me their assessment of Levi's condition. With furrowed brows and downturned mouths, they grimly informed us that his body was working to fight off infection and his organs were being severely taxed. If he survived, they told me, he would need multiple amputations. A host of fatal complications, like blood infections and organ failure, was possible. Despite their broken English, I heard them loud and clear: This baby's chances for survival were minimal at best. Tears welled up in my eyes and my heart sank. I tried to focus on what the doctors were saying, but all I could think was, *Please, God, don't make him hurt anymore.*

By their estimations, Levi would probably lose one arm, both hands, and possibly both feet. The thought of him not having hands or feet made me cringe. What kind of life will this child have if he can't even perform the most basic physical functions? How will he feed himself, dress himself, use the toilet, or play with toys and friends? With scars on his face and body he would never live a day without people staring at him. He would face constant questions. As my fatalistic tendencies and fears washed over me, I felt breathless and panicky. I knew God could heal this baby, but the clock was ticking. I'm no doctor, but even I could tell that the Langfang hospital was not equipped to provide the kind of intensive burn treatment he needed.

Then and there I determined I was going to do whatever it took to ensure this baby did not have to face a life like the one I had just imagined. Emily and I blew kisses through the glass as we said good-bye to Levi that morning. As soon as I returned home, I set to work on finding him better treatment options. Several hours later I learned that the Beijing Children's Hospital had a good burn unit. I asked our staff to phone the hospital to see about getting Levi transferred for treatment. Through translators I pleaded with them to let Levi come to their hospital for treatment. "We have one available bed," the woman at the admitting office told me, "but you have to get the baby here by 10 P.M. or we won't be able to take him."

Burns are common in China, especially among children,

and beds at the burn center fill quickly. I knew that if Levi didn't take the bed that night, the opportunity would be lost and his last chance would have slipped away.

I was driven to keep Levi alive no matter what it took. I kept thinking, *If this were my child, I'd want him to have the best care possible.* Getting him to Beijing seemed like his only hope for survival, but pulling this off would be an enormous feat.

I called the Langfang hospital to tell them I wanted to transfer Levi. It felt like slamming into a brick wall when the doctor said, "We refuse to release this baby. In his fragile state, we're afraid transporting him will kill him." Faced with this catch-22—if I don't get him to Beijing, Levi will die; if I transport him, he may die—I weighed my options. Death was nearly certain if he stayed in Langfang. While moving him to a new hospital was risky, at least I would know we had done everything we could. With new resolve, I called the doctor back. "I insist on moving Levi to Beijing," I said in no uncertain terms.

"Absolutely not," he retorted.

The Chinese are typically a gentle, soft-spoken people. But when push comes to shove and a verbal showdown ensues, you can count on them to fight to the end. My forceful demeanor was not winning any allies at the hospital. I realized that I may have unwittingly just cost Levi his life. I knew that by 10 P.M. that night, if he wasn't at the hospital in Beijing, his life would be over.

As a foreign woman on an unfamiliar playing field, I faced doctors who had the home-field advantage. I hung up the phone with the Langfang hospital feeling utterly dejected and hopeless. *How can I get him out of there?* my mind raced. *Who can help me save this baby?*

Running out of time and with no other viable options to pursue, I reluctantly headed to a dinner meeting that had been planned that night with our team. We were meeting some Chinese officials and a well-connected businessman named Mr. Sun to explore the possibility of purchasing land on which to add more foster homes.

When I got to the restaurant, I was depressed about Levi and didn't really want to be there. Mr. Sun noticed my downcast mood and asked, "Lisa, what's happening with that baby I saw today?" John had taken Mr. Sun to see Levi that morning and said that he was moved by Levi's distress. Not wanting to get off point with the meeting, one of our teammates jumped in and said, "This is a business meeting. We shouldn't be talking about this right now."

"Yes, we should discuss it," Mark Wei, interrupted. "It's significant."

"The Langfang hospital refuses to release him to Beijing," I explained. "If we don't get him there by 10 P.M., they will give up the only bed they have available. And if we don't get him there tonight, I don't think Levi will survive."

Moved by my despair for Levi, Mr. Sun said, "I know the head of the Langfang hospital, and I know the ambulance driver. Let me make a few phone calls." To my surprise, Mr. Sun took out his cell phone right there and called the top administrator of the hospital, explaining in rapid-fire Chinese our crisis. The next thing I knew, the Langfang hospital agreed to release Levi to Beijing, and an ambulance was preparing to transport him.

When we had finished our meal, John and I went back to the Bakers' house to gather the money we would need to pay the ambulance driver and the Beijing Children's Hospital for admitting Levi. In China, you often have to pay for medical care in advance. This took some getting used to. You had to pay for treatment first, wait for them to handwrite a receipt, and bring this down as proof of payment to the doctors before they would treat you.

Suddenly, we noticed flashing lights outside the windows. The ambulance had arrived! Through the back window, I could see Levi bundled up, his tiny body swaddled on a flat, baby-sized gurney. He looked peaceful and was taking a much-needed break from wailing.

The drive to Beijing would take nearly an hour, and once at the hospital, he would need to be admitted. We needed someone from our team who could speak Chinese and English. Ironically, the same man who suggested we not discuss Levi's condition over dinner was given the task of accompanying him in the ambulance to the Beijing Children's Hospital.

Nothing else was ever accomplished by the business meeting that night. No property was purchased; none of the people present became players in the next project. It seemed the whole evening had been divinely orchestrated to bring together the right people at the right time who could help save Levi's life. If John had not brought Mr. Sun to the hospital earlier that day, he would not have become yet another link in the everexpanding chain of people and events that would lead to saving Levi.

This is something to remember, I thought. *No matter what happens tomorrow, we will remember and praise God for the joyful blessing he gave us this night!*

CHAPTER FOUR

Holding Vigil in Beijing

Surely the arm of the LORD is not too short to save,
nor his ear too dull to hear.

—ISAIAH 59:1

IN THE SPRING, THE GOBI DESERT is notorious for kicking up sand into violent storms. The prevailing winds pick up the storms and blow them all the way to Beijing where they obscure the sky with loamy deposits. Sometimes, when the wind blows especially hard, dust from the northern plains of the Gobi actually makes its way as far as the west coast of the United States. The Chinese government tried to address this problem with a campaign that provided trees along the border of the Gobi desert to serve as a barrier from these sandstorms. Apparently, the tree line wasn't doing its job on this particular day when Tim and I arrived at the

Beijing Children's Hospital to meet with Levi's doctors for his initial assessment. The sky was awash with orange silt.

Even in the short walk from the hospital's parking lot to the main entrance, we were dusted with reddish sand. We brushed off as we made our way to the room where they had saved a bed for Levi the night before. I was anxious to hear how he had done during his first night. *How had he fared alone in a strange place? Was he still in agony over his burns, or had they given him something strong for the pain?* With one night away from him, I was antsy to see how the little boy was doing. The nurses directed us into a large dormitory-style room rimmed by old incubators and worn-out cribs. The darkly painted, peeling walls and cold cement floors did little to soothe the eight other children who were recovering from or awaiting surgery.

Like the Langfang hospital, the Beijing Children's Hospital was not the cleanest. Judging by the dried blood on the incubator glass where they had placed Levi, another child had recently been treated here and they hadn't had time to clean up after his stay. Tim spotted a fly in his incubator and had to tell a nurse to get it out.

After a short wait, a tall, thin woman doctor entered the room and joined us alongside Levi's incubator. With little in the way of an introduction, she unwrapped the stethoscope from around her neck and performed a check of his vitals. His heartbeat had stabilized, and his breathing sounded clear. She situated the stethoscope boa-style around her neck, and staring at Levi, she got right to the point. Speaking in choppy English, she said, "Look at this baby. He's so badly burned. If he even survives, he'll never be anything. He's not even your child. Why do you want to save this baby? Why not just let nature take its course?"

At our orphanage, our whole mission is simply to take children as we find them, love and nurture them, and then provide whatever medical care they need to become physically healthy and adoptable. Levi was the most extreme expression of this philosophy. *How far are you really willing to go to live out this mission? Does it make sense to put limited resources into such a long shot? Is trying to save Levi like throwing good money after a lost cause?* These were the kinds of questions written on the faces of each doctor and nurse we met. It was as if the Chinese medical world wanted to test our resolve, to provide us a medically sanctioned excuse to give up on Levi.

Tim's response was both gentle and powerful. He said that he wanted to see Levi grow up and graduate from school. He said he would be there on Levi's wedding day. If no one else wants to adopt him, then he would adopt him. When I heard Tim give this answer, I was proud of the way he responded. And yet I knew in my heart, it would not be Tim at the wedding. It would be John and I.

The doctor was not accustomed to seeing anyone care so much for an orphan, and a severely burned one at that. She stood there a moment considering what she was seeing and hearing, as if trying to understand the compassion she was witnessing.

"Okay," she said, "I think we can get him in for surgery within two or three days."

No! my heart told me. *If they wait, it will be too late!* "You have to operate right away," I insisted. "If you wait, his chances of survival will go down even further."

Seeing our determination, she finally acquiesced. Sighing, she said, "I'll see what we can do. Let me meet with my staff, and I'll let you know when we can schedule him in."

The doctor looked sorrowfully at Levi, nodded good-bye, and left Tim and me standing watch over him. We took turns cooing through the glass. It was too soon for either one of us to try to pick him up and hold him. Although he desperately needed comforting, any pressure against his damaged skin would hurt him.

We left the hospital to return to our families in Langfang. Although Levi had captured our attention, we still had our own children, other orphans, and plenty of work to do. Fund raising, operating the orphanage, buying supplies—the work never stopped.

The next day while John and Tim tackled the work at the orphanage, I returned to Beijing to visit Levi again. I spent the rest of the day listening to him and eight other children struggle in pain. The Chinese do not use pacifiers, and yet Levi desperately needed some way to comfort himself. I asked a doctor for a bottle nipple, and I stuffed it with gauze and slipped it in his mouth. Levi immediately sucked on it with all his strength. Aside from this momentary lapse of tranquility, cries rang out constantly in the dingy, noise-filled room, echoing off the cement floors. There were no bright colored posters of puppies or kittens to cheer the patients, no flowers or balloons.

The only bright spot was the nurses who dressed in pilgrim-style aprons layered over pastel cotton dresses topped off by white boat-shaped hats secured by bobby pins on top of their heads. Their old-fashioned uniforms evoked a sense of order and cleanliness—until you saw them up close and realized how faded they had become as a result of too many hard-water washings. Nonetheless, the nurses moved about the room with efficiency, and they showed a comforting tenderness toward their little charges. In China, nurses do not perform tasks like changing diapers or toileting older children, or providing feedings or meals for the patients. Parents or caregivers are expected to handle these duties, so along with the eight children in the room sat eight mothers, tending to their children's needs. Most looked downcast and sad as they struggled to know how to comfort their children.

I tried to communicate with the other mothers one by one. Unfortunately, having lived in China for only about one month, I spoke virtually no Chinese, and they spoke no English. They seemed intrigued by the fact that I was a white woman keeping watch over a Chinese boy. Though they couldn't put it into words, their eyes expressed the question, *Why is this foreign woman here caring for a burned Chinese infant?* All I could think was, *If they only knew the half of it!*

While I was trying to get to know my new neighbors, a welcome visitor stepped into the room. Sam Komakech walked toward me with a big smile and outstretched arms. Sam was an African doctor completing his residency hours at the nearby Beijing United Family Center. John and I had met Sam and his wife, Jay Jay, at the Beijing International Christian

Fellowship, the church where we and many other expatriate families worship. Sam spoke fluent Chinese and English, so we asked his help in communicating with the medical staff. His timing couldn't have been better, because just after he arrived, a new doctor asked to meet with us in her office. This doctor was soft-spoken and kindhearted. She demonstrated a genuine concern for Levi and explained about the surgeries Levi would need and what the risks were.

The doctor opened her file and presented me with a packet of waivers to sign. She explained to Sam in Chinese the risks associated with surgery. She was compassionate but clear: Levi would probably not survive this surgery. Sam translated. Every death scenario sounded just as ominous in Chinese as it did in English. He was an infant with too many body parts open and at risk for infection. There was a good chance given his young age and the trauma he had endured, that he would go into shock from the surgery. Also, because he was only about six weeks old, he faced the risk of losing too much blood. Skin grafts are messy, bloody surgeries. In his compromised state, Levi couldn't afford to lose any more blood or other body fluids. Seventy percent of his body was burned. This meant there would be minimal skin from his own body to harvest, and it was highly likely he would reject donor skin. Essentially, they were going to have to scalp him and use his head skin to patch up his body. There was a chance he might always be bald from this.

Who cares if he's bald, I thought, *I just want this baby to live.*

Although I was grateful that the doctors were willing to proceed with an unprecedented Saturday surgery, I was in a somber mood after signing off on the all the waivers. *Am I signing this boy's death sentence, or offering him a new lease on life?* It would be 24 hours before I would know the answer to this question.

With tears in my eyes, I thanked Sam for taking the time to translate for me. I realized that his visit wasn't just serendipity; it was salvation. Sam had become another link in the chain of kindness that continued to bind Levi together with people from around the world.

救

After saying our good-byes, I headed back to Levi's room. As I peered at him through the glass and considered the risks that lay ahead for him the next day, it suddenly occurred to me: *This might be his last day alive.* He was facing major surgery, and the doctors were giving him only a slight chance of survival, much less successful recovery. If this were his last night on earth, I didn't want him to be alone. So I called John and explained the situation. "I just can't come home tonight," I said. "I'm going to stay with Levi."

Joining the eight other mothers lined up in straight-back chairs next to their babies' beds, I pulled up the well-worn seat assigned to my space. *How many other mothers have sat in this chair, pleading for their babies' lives?*

As I surveyed the room, I noticed that all of the parents had brought their own meals in plastic bags, along with food for their sick children. Levi was being fed formula in a bottle, which the nurse did bring to me every few hours so that I could feed him. Except for when he was sucking down his bottle, Levi cried incessantly. When he tried to move his arm, ashes would fall from it. I never got used to this sight. To see a baby in so much pain—all I could think was, *God, no human strength can save him. We need a miracle from You.*

Chinese mothers make a different kind of calming sound when nurturing their children. Theirs is a very comforting coo, which suggests sympathy—"Uuh, uuh, uuh." This worked to quiet all the babies in the room, except for Levi. For hours, he writhed in pain, only occasionally breaking when he heard me sing quietly or read from the Bible. Shortly after we moved to China, I lost the Bible I had used for years, so Pam Baker had thoughtfully just brought me one from Hong Kong. As the afternoon light faded into darkness, I sat with Levi in the dim room, flipping pages and letting my Bible fall open. I picked random verses from whatever page I landed on. Verses seemed to leap off the pages, verses like Matthew 13:44: "The kingdom of heaven is like treasure that was hidden in a field" (NIRV). But it was portions of Psalm 118 that left me stunned and filled with the realization that God planned not only to save Levi, but to use his story as a testimony for others:

> When I was in great pain, I cried out to the LORD.
> He answered me and set me free.
> The LORD is with me. I will not be afraid.
> What can mere men do to me?
> The LORD is with me. He helps me. . . .
> I was pushed back. I was about to be killed.

But the LORD helped me.

The LORD gives me strength. I sing about him.

He has saved me. . . .

[They shout,] "The LORD's powerful right hand has
    won the battle!

The LORD's powerful right hand has done mighty things!"

I will not die. I will live.

I will talk about what the LORD has done. . . .

You are my God, and I will give thanks to you.

You are my God, and I will honor you.

Give thanks to the LORD, because he is good.

His faithful love continues forever.

    (verses 5-7, 13-14, 16-17, 28-29, NIRV)

After I read those words, I realized that despite the doctors' prediction that he would have a poor life, God had a very different plan for Levi. He would have a vibrant and powerful life. Whatever God's plan was, I got the distinct feeling He was directing me to praise Him in advance for saving this little boy who had been left to die but whom God had destined to live.

救

The doctors weren't giving Levi anything stronger than Tylenol. He was in such pain, and it was breaking my heart. Not only that, he kept trying to root around for something to suckle on, the way a nursing baby does. Several times I noticed him bringing his charred little thumb near his mouth as if he wanted to suck it, but he would always stop short as if some instinct told him that what used to soothe him was part of his past and he could never use his thumb again.

I couldn't help but imagine the agony he must have felt lying in that field, watching his mother walk away. She was his only source of food. All life came from her. I have given birth to four babies and nursed each one, so I know the bond that quickly develops between a mother and her child. Somewhere in or near the village of Langfang was a mother who was experiencing the pain of not being able to nurse her baby. Every nursing mom knows how uncomfortably full you get when you can't release the milk that nature continues to produce after you've had a baby. There was no doubt in my mind that this discomfort was serving as a heartbreaking reminder to Levi's biological mother that her baby was gone. And lest anyone would discover her secret—that she abandoned her baby in a field—this mother was silently suffering a grief I could not imagine.

While I was maintaining my vigil beside Levi's incubator, the nurses told me that a room had just opened up next to their workstation. You would have thought I had just been offered the presidential suite at a five-star hotel. Quietly, so as not to disturb the babies who had managed to fall asleep, the nurses wheeled Levi's incubator out of the shared room into the much quieter, although equally dingy, private room. What a relief to have a break from the communal-care room where the babies' crying set off a continual chain reaction of wailing.

I was wound up from the stress of not being able to comfort Levi in his pain; all I could do was sit on the edge of my bed and continue to watch and pray for him. In the middle of the night while I was feeding Levi a bottle, a doctor stopped in to see how we were doing. As she examined Levi briefly, I accidentally dropped the bottle. The doctor picked it up off the floor and, without even rinsing it off, plugged it into Levi's mouth. As he talked, I pulled the bottle out and wiped off the nipple before giving it back to him. *Boy, they must not realize how many germs there are on floors.* The doctor proceeded to give Levi another dose of acetaminophen, hoping this would help take the edge off his pain. He nodded good-bye, and left Levi and me to ourselves, wide awake, with Levi concentrating on his pain and me thinking about the surgery that was now just hours away.

Levi and I were still awake when morning finally came. The nurses asked me to wheel Levi out of our private room and back into the big dorm room. Positioned in the middle of the room and by the door were two common sinks where older children could wash up and brush their teeth. No one was afforded the luxury of privacy. The other mothers were tenderly caring for their children, feeding them, cleaning and getting them dressed, or changing diapers.

And while the other parents were busy with their own children, Levi remained the object of curiosity. He was by far the most seriously injured child. One kindly man who spoke some English encouraged me and shared his hope that Levi would have a successful surgery.

I knew these Chinese parents were doing the best they could for their children. They sweetly tried to communicate with me again, and in spite of the language barrier that stood like a tree line between us, the winds of understanding still managed to blow through.

Today was Saturday, the day of Levi's first life-saving surgery. It was not customary for the Beijing Children's Hospital to operate on weekends, but I knew if they didn't, Levi's chance for survival would drop from very bad to nonexistent. It had been a long journey from the Langfang hospital to the Beijing Children's Hospital, and although I feared for Levi, I was relieved that this day had arrived. I was filled with gratitude toward the entire hospital staff for coming together as a team, bending policies and making a way to pull off this last-minute surgery.

The nurses entered the room and cautiously moved him from his incubator onto an adult-sized gurney. I walked alongside the rolling bed as far as the operating room. At this point, they motioned for me to remain outside. I watched as they wheeled Levi through the double doors. As soon as they swung shut, fear once again hit me like a gust of red sand: *These could be Levi's last moments on earth!* I ran through the doors and motioned to the nurses to stop for a moment. I wanted to see him one more time before I said good-bye. With a sadness for the fight this little boy would need to wage for his life, I whispered a prayer under my breath: "Please, God, save Levi."

Reluctantly, I left the operating room and headed back into the room where I had spent the previous night holding vigil over Levi's incubator. Seeing it empty now, I knelt down beside it in sadness. *Will this become an empty tomb, forever marking this as the day Levi returned to the land of the living—or will it become a coffin, the place they will lay him if surgery doesn't turn out right?*

CHAPTER FIVE

From Beijing to Boston

Love recognizes no barriers. It jumps hurdles, leaps fences,
penetrates walls to arrive at its destination full of hope.
—MAYA ANGELOU

救

EXHAUSTED AND HUNGRY, I decided to take a quick break and get some breakfast across the street at McDonald's. Even though I knew the surgery would take hours to complete, I didn't want to be gone long. I rushed through my meal and walked back into the building where Levi's life was now in someone else's hands. I found a row of attached plastic chairs, four rows deep, in the burn unit waiting room and I planted myself for about five hours.

With little sleep to keep my mind focused, my thoughts drifted back in time to another day when I found myself sitting in a waiting room similar to this one. I was about three years old, and hot coffee had spilled down the right side of my body, leaving me with third-degree burns on my arm. The problem with burns is the pain doesn't end when the event is over. The sharp pain continued long after the coffee was washed off. Only the comfort of my dad sitting next to me and holding me eased my suffering. Levi still had never known this kind of comfort. How I longed for the day I could hold him without making his pain worse. Not yet having a father of his own, he did not know the security that comes from having a bigger, stronger man scoop him into his arms and make whatever is wrong in the world seem right in that instant.

Memories of the past morphed into prayers for the present—prayers for the baby boy who needed comfort and protection right now. It's funny how effortlessly prayer flowed from me now, considering that I didn't really pick up on the habit until I was an adult. Growing up, when people would ask me what my religion was, I would always say, "Half Jewish, half Christian." I felt a closer connection with my Jewish father and his relatives because they had a sense of community and they were involved in each other's lives.

My father's family was Jewish by ethnicity and not in faith. Being Jewish to him was more about the culture, the relationships, and the community. Although I prided myself on being Jewish, saying I was half Jewish and half Christian started feeling like I had only half a faith. At some point, I decided I wanted more. My mom had planted seeds of prayer in my life when she taught us the Lord's Prayer, and occasionally on Easter she would take me and my two brothers to a Lutheran church. It took many more years and lots of hard knocks for this mustard seed to turn into a mature plant.

Before I could wind down memory lane any further, the operating room doors flung open. Though nearly five hours had gone by, it seemed like no time had passed. As soon as she saw me, the surgeon announced, "Levi is alive!" as she and a team of doctors wheeled Levi out in a big rolling hospital bed. She told me that in the history of the burn center there had never been a baby so young and so severely burned who survived. Not wanting to encourage my hope too much, she subdued her excitement by reminding me in broken English that he wasn't out of danger yet.

I didn't listen then; I was too happy he had survived. Levi was wrapped head to toe like a mummy. The doctors had been conservative on the amputations, not wanting to take more than absolutely necessary. They had removed part of his left arm and excised all of the charred wounds on his body. They attempted some skin grafts using the skin from his head. The doctors made no promises for his recovery, but in those first few moments, I was filled with hope. I couldn't wait to get home to share the good news.

My initial exuberance lasted about as long as a Roman candle on the Fourth of July. The next day, what had shot up in a shower of sparks and balls of fire now, upon news from the doctor, fizzled and faded disappointingly. Overnight, Levi was besieged by a blood infection that was aggressively attacking his system. The day before I had only seen him all wrapped up like a mummy; I didn't realize how frail and traumatized his little body really was from the surgery. It was clear now by the doctor's grim update that he was in serious distress. I knew the Beijing doctors were doing all they could to save Levi, but it became apparent in that instant that it wasn't going to be enough.

Within two days, Levi's body had rejected the skin grafts and his blood infection was jeopardizing his life. The doctors needed to amputate farther up Levi's left arm. The orphanage authorized a second round of surgery with great sadness. It felt like I was losing Levi limb by limb. It was bad enough he would face a life with scars all over his body, but with each amputation, he would also lose a part of his autonomy.

I pondered Levi's future as I awaited news on the success of his second surgery. A couple of hours later, a team of doctors exited the operating room and brought an update. The amputation had gone smoothly, but now they needed to focus on stabilizing him. The infections had exacted a huge toll on his body. I knew then that Levi's recovery was anything but a sure thing. Like hot lava seeping over mountain rocks, infection was overtaking his extremities and killing off more and more tissue. With every day that went by, he risked losing another hand, another toe. It didn't look like his body would be able to fight back.

Behind the scenes, everyone involved with the orphanage was trying to enlist prayer and financial support for Levi. His medical expenses were mounting, and we still had about two dozen other orphans in our care with urgent—although not life-threatening—needs.

I called a meeting with our team at the orphanage later that day. "What else can we do for Levi?" I asked John, Tim, and Mark. "The Beijing doctors are doing the best they can, but there's got to be more we can do."

Tim told me about an e-mail he had received from a doctor in Boston. Dr. John Schulz was the head of the burn unit at Shriners Hospitals for Children–Boston. One of the thousands of supporters who had received Tim's first e-mail had forwarded Levi's picture and prayer request to Dr. Schulz to see if he could help. Dr. Schulz had adopted a daughter from China years earlier. When he saw the picture John had taken the first day, Dr. Schulz could not resist the call for help. He had sent Tim a reply saying he would help in any way he could.

Desperate for any lead that might provide a lifeline for Levi, I e-mailed Dr. Schulz back that night. I tried to describe in laymen's terms the treatment Levi had received to that point. Levi was dying, and time was not on our side. I e-mailed Dr. Schulz asking, "Would you come to China to save Levi's life?"

Dr. Schulz responded almost immediately and said, "If the Beijing Children's Hospital will give me authority to operate in their facility, I'll consider coming to China to help save his life."

This was all the hope I needed. To think that there was a doctor an ocean away, willing to leave his family for a boy he had never met—I was overwhelmed to think of this stranger's compassion. Thinking about Levi now, mummy-wrapped and with his arm being whittled away by each surgery, I decided that the best scenario would be to get him to the United States for treatment. Shriners Hospitals for Children–Boston has a state-of-the-art burn center. Doctors there perform surgeries on burn patients throughout the New England region, and whenever possible, they assist families like ours from overseas by providing free care. This gives their doctors the opportunity to hone their skills and utilize the equipment they've invested in.

Having Dr. Schulz assist the doctors in Beijing would be a great step toward improving Levi's chances for survival. But getting him to Boston would be best. The level of care they offered far surpassed what Levi was receiving in Beijing.

But there would be many hurdles to get through in order to take that route. How in the world would we get an undocumented Chinese baby into the United States? The odds of our being able to get all of the necessary paperwork completed, not to mention plane tickets, a place for me to stay in Boston, plus a caregiver for the months following his surgeries were slim to none. My heart started racing just considering all of the obstacles. *God, this is our only hope of saving this baby. Please, help us.*

I had fought for a lot of underdogs in my life, but at that moment, Levi's match against time and circumstances was the most heavily weighted fight I had ever encountered. If it weren't for the fact that rooting for underdogs is my specialty, I might have looked at Levi's circumstances and decided he was too much of a long shot. Instead, I decided to focus on

July 2006—Levi sits in the field where he was abandoned as an infant.

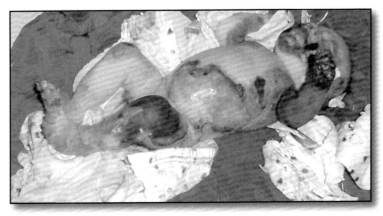

March 14, 2002—Levi with the blanket and burial clothes he was wearing the night he was found

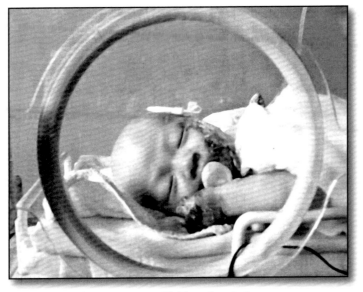

Levi in an incubator at Beijing Childrens hospital

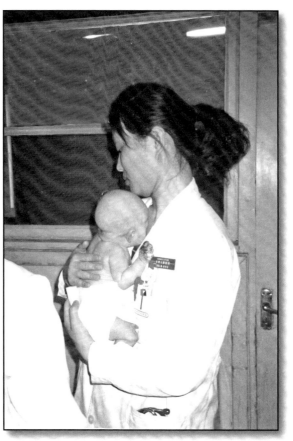

Dr. Li Hi Xia at Beijing Children's Hospital comforts Levi the day before his first surgery.

Levi in bandages after his first surgery

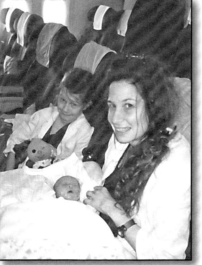

Emily, Lisa, and Levi on a United Airlines flight to Boston for Levi's "miracle" surgery

Lisa and Dr. John Schultz, of Shriners Hospitals for Children–Boston

Levi at Shriners Hospitals for Children–Boston surrounded by a germ-free tent

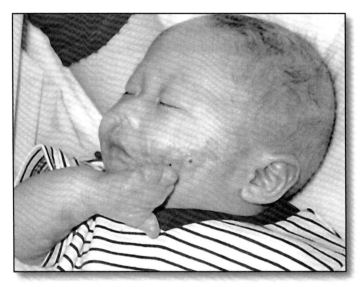

*Levi shortly after his first
U.S. surgery*

Levi, age 10 months

*Levi, age 4, holding a baby bootie
he was wearing the day he was
found in the field*

United Airlines flight attendant Sara Ritter with Levi, 10 months, and Lisa on the second flight to Boston.

August 2002—Lisa at Shriners Hospitals for Children–Boston with Levi's surgeon, Dr. Rob Sheridan

Special visitors for Levi at the Beijing United Family Hospital (from left to right): U.S. Ambassador to China Clark Randt Jr., Levi, John, former Secretary of Health and Human Services Tommy Thompson, Lisa. (Front row from left to right): *Orly, Emily, and Ian Bentley.*

Pastor John Cowan and his wife, Laura, of Calvary Chapel in Sacramento, California, visit Levi at Shriners Hospitals for Children– Northern California in 2003. The Cowans provided housing for the Bentleys during their stay for Levi's surgery. Left to right: *Laura Cowan, Levi, John Cowan, Ian, Lisa and Emily.*

Below: *Levi following surgery at Shriners Hospitals for Children– Northern California*

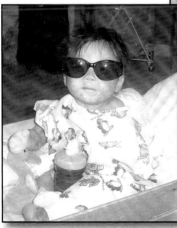

Above: *October 2003—Carole Blackshaw, Lady Mayoress of London, 2002–2003, holding Levi during a visit to the Langfang orphanage*

Levi as a toddler, holding his uncle Tony's hand

Emily, age 12, with Levi, age 2, in Langfang

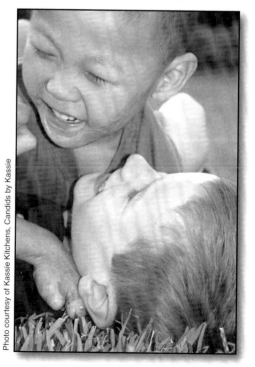

Levi, age 4, wrestling in the grass with Oliver, age 7

Levi, age 3, with Donald "Reid," age 4

Cynthia Qiu, United Airlines marketing specialist, with Levi, age 4

Reunion with Beijing United Airlines sales and marketing team that helped facilitate the "miracle" flight to Boston (from left to right): Michael Ching, Mary Ma, Levi, Cynthia Qiu and Lisa

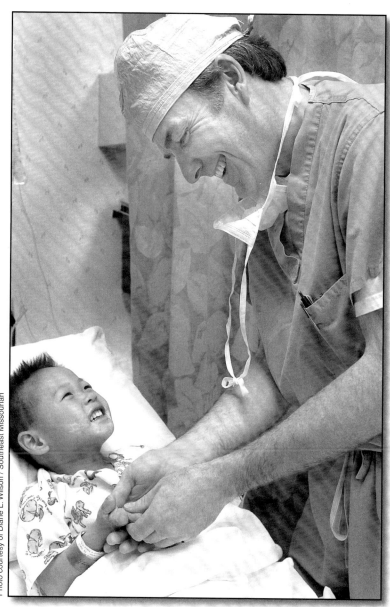

April 2006—Levi with Dr. Gregory Tobin, who performed facial surgery on Levi at Auburn Surgery Center in Cape Girardeau, Missouri

Levi with Beth Carter, a nurse at Auburn Surgery Center in Cape Girardeau, Missouri

*Summer 2006—*From left to right: *Donald "Reid," Oliver, Emily, Lisa, Levi, Ian, John and Orly*

Summer 2006—Levi, back home in China

Levi, age 3½

At Beijing Capital International Airport. Back row, left to right: *Emily, Levi, Andrea Lucado, Nancy Bode (a United Airlines flight attendant on the first "miracle" flight to Boston), Lisa, John.* Front row, left to right: *Donald "Reid," Orly, Ian, and Oliver*

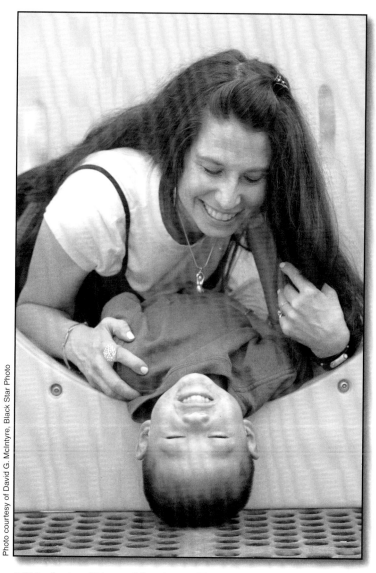

2006—Levi and Lisa with her shu *necklace*

And so my prayer is that your story will have involved some leaving and some coming home, some summer and some winter . . . My hope is your story will be about changing . . . about learning to love a child . . . about learning to love others more than we love ourselves . . . We get one story, you and I, and one story alone. God has established the elements, the setting and the climax and the resolution. It would be a crime not to venture out, wouldn't it? . . . And you will not be alone. You have never been alone. Don't worry. Everything will still be here when you get back. It is you who will have changed. —DONALD MILLER, THROUGH PAINTED DESERTS what God could accomplish. I would not rest until I had done everything I could to step in and help this defenseless little boy.

I wasn't the only one who had been looking out for Levi. Since the day we had first received Levi into our care, Mark had been working behind the scenes to get Levi documented and registered. Mr. Yan, the director of the Langfang Orphanage, had gone with Mark to the police station the day after we brought Levi to the hospital. Typically, when a baby is found abandoned, the police need to register the baby's *hukou*, or permanent residence. This takes some time to complete, because before the police sign off on the *hukou*, they first do an investigation to try to find the parents and determine whether or not the baby has really been abandoned. The law requires that an advertisement be placed in the newspapers for a few weeks asking for information on the lost child to allow for parents to step forward. If there is no response, then the child is declared abandoned.

Typically it is months before a *hukou* is issued. When Mr. Yan and Mark arrived at the police station that next day, the police officer was absent, so they could not file for Levi's registration. By the time they finally were able to meet with the officer, Levi was already being transferred to Beijing for surgery. "If you spend any time trying to investigate what happened to this baby, his life will be over," Mark explained to the officer. "We're asking you to expedite his *hukou* so that we can get him the treatment he needs."

The officer considered Mark's request. He looked over the letter Mark had presented from the China Charity Federation.

In it, they validated the work we were doing by saying we were a good and capable organization and able to care for Levi. The police officer set down the letter and picked up the phone. After making a couple of phone calls, he told Mark in Chinese, "I will issue you the baby's *hukou*." This unprecedented move gave us a giant head start in getting Levi permission to leave the country. With his Chinese residency registration in hand, Mark puzzled over what steps to take next. With new resolve and a vision for how we could save Levi, I knew the next step. "We need to work on getting Levi to America," I said. "Can you help?"

Mark responded, "Frankly, I don't know how to send a Chinese orphan to America. I have to figure out how to do this. I believe something is going on behind all this, though. So far, everyone I meet wants to do something for Levi. People's hearts are touched by his little life."

Mark is a man of deep faith. In all of the years he worked with Tim in setting up CBN's China office, Mark helped CBN gain entrance into China where no others had been able to before. If anyone could figure out how to make a way through the labyrinth of Chinese government, Mark could.

He set to work immediately. Armed with the letter from the China Charity Foundation, he drove over to the Ministry of Civil Affairs office to request permission to let Levi leave China for medical treatment. They gave us a green light to take Levi out of the country, but even with permission granted, there was still the issue of how to get Levi a passport and visa on such short notice. This would require going through both the

Chinese Ministry of Civil Affairs and the U.S. embassy for approval, which easily could take six weeks or longer. We desperately needed a way to speed up this process.

With each Chinese ministry visit, Mark was given instructions on where to go next to continue the documentation process. Mark spent day after day driving from one office to the next describing Levi's medical emergency and our goal in getting him treatment at Shriners Hospitals for Children–Boston. Every time Mark shared Levi's story, people responded to his plea for help. They were touched by the plight of this little boy and our willingness to save him, and Chinese officials responded in kind with an eagerness to do their part.

While Mark burned the candle on one end in a life-or-death paper chase, I was burning the candle on the other end trying to figure out the logistics of how to physically get Levi to Boston. I had left Levi in the care of some wonderful women from a local Chinese church so that I could go home and spend time with John and the kids. Their mission was to provide daily, round-the-clock caregiving at the hospital for families who could not stay at the hospital with their children. These women tenderly cared for and prayed over Levi in my absence. They also changed his diapers, fed him his bottles, and offered as much comfort to him as they could. Although I missed spending so much time by Levi's bedside, I gratefully abdicated this position, knowing the best I could do for Levi now was to work tirelessly on getting him out of the country. Thankfully, we also had hired a Chinese nanny who took care of most of the housekeeping duties, like cleaning and laundry.

I was supposed to be home-schooling Emily, Ian, and Oliver, but all of that was on hold now. Even when I was home, I spent most of my time on the phone or on my computer, e-mailing every person I could think of who might provide a missing link to Levi's survival. If we were going to get him out of the country, we would need to work every angle and use every friendship we had to make it happen.

The intensity of my mission stopped only long enough for lunch breaks. Because we were still so new to China, on most days I would take the kids to the local Chinese restaurant. I spent hours each day trying to connect with people and organizations in radically different time zones that might be able to help us. When I first became involved with our orphanage a few months earlier, Tim had given me a book from AmCham, the American Chinese Chamber of Commerce, which lists all of the American companies doing business in China. I had contacted three people in this book to try to raise funds for the little orphanage at Langfang. At the time, many people on our team viewed my efforts with skepticism, and I even received criticism for it. *Why would a Christian organization go outside of the community for assistance,* they wondered. *Shouldn't we ask only Christians for help?*

This attitude didn't square with my experience of how God operates. Even in the few short weeks since I had fallen in love with Levi, God's chain of "miracles" included many non-Christian "links." Who's to say God wasn't using Levi as a means to bring about greater good?

It turned out the phone calls I had made previously became

lifesaving connections for Levi now. The man who was the president of Baby Care Ltd., Matthew Estes, also happened to be a Christian. When I made my initial contact with him on behalf of the orphanage, he had generously agreed to donate baby food. Matthew told two ladies at his church about Levi. Because of his promptings, each of these women contacted us to see how they could help with Levi. One of these women happened to be connected with the American embassy. She became a key contact in our desperate efforts to get Levi a passport and proper documentation to and from Boston for surgery.

The other woman was Nancy Fraser. In the six years she had lived in China, Nancy had developed relationships with people in all walks of life, many of whom she used to help get Levi what he needed. So from this one AmCham phone call I had made a month earlier, I was now reaping a harvest of help I never could have imagined.

Still, even with such good fortune in getting the details squared away, each day Levi was losing strength, and my home life was falling apart. In between my daily quest for ways to get Levi to Boston, I tried to sneak in visits to the hospital to see him. This added nearly three hours onto my already full day.

Making my children memorize math facts seemed far less important in the face of Levi's life-and-death situation. Dust had started to accumulate on their schoolbook covers. Family meals also had become a distant memory. We gobbled down food when and where we could in the course of our days. In too many ways, all our kids—and John—were getting was leftovers. Like a tea kettle that had been simmering on the stove, it was only a matter of time before the water boiled over and the whistle started to scream. The lid finally blew off at the end of one particularly long, arduous day. I don't recall the specific details that pushed us over the edge, but I do remember John standing in the middle of our yucky living room (we hadn't moved to the new house yet), the sound of rats scratching behind the walls like fingernails on a chalkboard only heightening the tension. "Lisa," he said, "you have four kids at home. Levi is taking you away from your own family too much. You are putting too much into all of this."

His words stung. *Isn't this the reason John brought me to China?* Even so, I couldn't dispute what John was telling me. Emily, Ian, Oliver, and Donald "Reid" had had to adapt to life in a strange culture. They came to China with two parents, but now it was as if they were being abandoned on a daily basis. From the time they were born, I had never left them. I had never worked outside our home; I never had hobbies that took me away from home. My whole life had consisted of taking care of them. Suddenly, they were forced to share me with someone else—a dying baby. The kids were extremely compassionate toward Levi and his suffering, but this didn't negate the fact that they had needs too. I tried to take John's words to heart and find a better balance between time spent saving Levi and time spent with my family. The reality was we just had to keep moving with Levi. Stopping would have meant his death. Every day I saw him in the hospital confirmed in my heart and mind that Levi was losing strength.

I knew my assessment was accurate the day I bumped into

the doctor who had given me all the waivers to sign before surgery. I was walking down the hall after checking in on Levi. As I passed by her, she looked up from her paperwork and said in surprisingly fluent English, "Lisa, if that baby survives, it will be your God who saves him."

Anyone else might have felt defeated by her words. But for me they lit a fire. I became obsessed with saving Levi. I asked Sam, our African doctor friend, to draft a letter to Dr. Schulz in Boston describing Levi's medical condition. I wanted Dr. Schulz to be as prepared as possible to treat him, trusting we would find a way to get Levi there.

One week earlier I had met Dr. Jane Liedtke at a professional women's meeting. She had been another one of my previous AmCham phone contacts. Little did I know at the time I first called her she would hold the key I needed to unlock the mystery of how to get Levi to America. Jane runs an organization called Our Chinese Daughters Foundation, which supports families that have adopted children from China. They also provide extensive trip planning for families traveling to China. When I told her about Levi and the obstacle I was facing getting him to Boston, she suggested I call the airlines and ask if they could help provide tickets for me to get to Boston with Levi. It was such a simple suggestion, but it provided the breakthrough I needed.

I zoomed home from the meeting that day and pulled out the phone book and started cold-calling airlines. "Hi, my name is Lisa Bentley. I run a foster home in Langfang, China, and I'm working on getting a severely burned baby to Boston for a lifesaving surgery. Can you help?" The first caller listened politely to my pitch, but then flatly said, "No, we can't help."

Feeling like I was swimming upstream against a powerful current, I dialed the next number. "Hi, my name is Lisa Bentley . . ." Again, I appealed for help, only to be rejected. "We don't offer this kind of assistance," the voice at the other end informed me. "Thanks for your time," I said sadly as I hung up, defeated a second time. *How am I going to get high enough up the chain of command to get a "yes"?* I prayed for a miracle.

Going to the airlines and asking for free tickets started to seem like a ridiculous approach. *Who would just give me free tickets?* I thought. *Airlines probably get requests like this all the time. No wonder they have to say no.* Defeat was sapping whatever shred of emotional strength I had left. Next on my list was United Airlines. I was feeling like Eeyore. Even though I was physically and emotionally exhausted, I decided to forge ahead and make one last call before giving up. The phone rang twice before Cynthia Qiu, a marketing specialist at United Airlines, answered.

"I don't want to waste your time; I don't want to waste my time," I bluntly told Cynthia after explaining who I was. "I've got a dying baby who I need to get on a plane from Beijing to Boston. Can you help me?"

Stunned by my abrupt introduction, Cynthia asked for a few more details. After hearing Levi's full story, I could tell she was choked up on the other end of the line. "I'll do whatever I can to help get Levi to Boston," she said softly through her tears. Now it was my turn to choke up. I couldn't believe this complete stranger, who I initially had no confidence would help me, had become the only difference between Levi's living and dying. Cynthia would need to jump through a lot of hoops to get approval for Levi's flight. Her helping us was a long shot, but it was the only hope I had at that point.

Meanwhile, Mark Wei had encountered other problems on his paper chase that could make plane tickets irrelevant. It took only days instead of weeks for Mark to complete all of the basic documentation and registration for Levi. The daunting task facing him now was how to get Levi a passport and visa— and fast! First, Mark needed to submit a photograph of Levi for his passport. Because he was so severely injured, there was no way we could bring him into the police station where one is normally required to have his passport picture taken. Mark had only a digital head shot of Levi taken in his incubator after the doctor at the Langfang hospital had smeared on white ointment. Levi looked like a baby with a beard of shaving cream.

"I assure you," Mark insisted to the police, "this is the actual baby." After debating whether or not they could accept Levi's picture, the police officer finally gave Mark the *chop*, or notary seal, he needed to submit our application for the passport and move on to the next round. Next, Mark sent all of Levi's information electronically to the Provincial Administration of Public Security Bureau.

The Provincial Administration of Public Security Bureau, or provincial police, would be responsible for approving or denying Levi's passport application. Faced with more red tape and knowing the clock was ticking, Mark implored the

Langfang police to help him. "Will you call the provincial police and ask them to issue the passport?" he begged. From this point, even in a best-case scenario, it would still be at least three weeks before we would have Levi's passport in hand.

In an uncommon act of grace, the Langfang police bureau made the call for Mark and asked the provincial police to issue the passport immediately. Mark breathed a silent prayer of thanks. Never before had the Langfang police been so willing to help. The provincial police agreed to expedite the passport, but they hinted that there might be problems that would slow them down. Mark decided to board a bus that evening and take care of the passport in person. Alone, he traveled to Shijiazhuang, the capital city of Hebei, a province southwest of Beijing.

When he walked in the next morning, Levi's passport was ready. A miracle! But just as the police officer extended the passport to Mark, he hesitated. "We need proof of kinship," the officer said. "Without it, we can't give you this passport."

"Proof of kinship?" Mark questioned, flustered by this last-minute deal breaker. "This baby is an orphan, and I am working to help save his life." The officer sized up Mark with a skeptical glance. Levi's life rested in the palm of his hand.

When my phone rang that morning, I had hoped it would be news from either Cynthia Qiu or Mark Wei. Instead, it was a doctor at the Beijing Children's Hospital. Levi had another blood infection, she informed me. "We're going to need to amputate his other arm," she said.

My heart stopped. *Dear God,* I thought, *he's not going to have any hands.*

I was frantic, thinking of how severely handicapped Levi might become. I told the doctor not to do anything yet, but I wasn't sure she had understood me. Too sad to know what else to say, I hung up and sat on the edge of my bed, stunned by this latest blow. *How many more obstacles will we have to face before getting this kid to Boston where he has a chance at living?*

Minutes later, Cynthia Qiu called. With excitement in her voice, she proclaimed, "We can get Levi to Boston!"

I quickly relayed this good news to John and Tim. They shared my excitement, but immediately asked two practical questions: "Where are you going to stay? Who will be Levi's caretaker when you return to China?"

"I don't know the answers," I said. "But I know that if God parted the Red Sea to get Levi to Boston, then He will take care of us." Witnessing provision after provision built up my faith. I had come a long way from my former self—a Woody Allen type character who believed everything was going to kill me.

Sponsoring tickets from United Airlines required management approval first, and when Cynthia attempted to bring our request up the chain of command, everyone was out of town. "I contacted my marketing manager, Mr. Zhang Fan in Shanghai, and also the general manager of United China, Mr. Sidney

Kwok, who is in the States." Cynthia explained excitedly. "Even with the time difference in the U.S. I got all of the approvals within a few hours." This was an incredible breakthrough, but my joy was tempered by the depressing phone call from the doctor. *How are we going to save Levi's arm?*

I barely formed the thought when my phone rang again. This time it was Mark. "Good news! We have everything we need to get Levi to America!" I was stunned. I had barely gotten out of bed, and already I had been assured plane tickets and Levi now had a passport and documentation to leave China and enter the United States. Energized by this good news, I was determined to tackle the remaining problem: How to stop the Chinese doctors from amputating any more of Levi's limbs.

In China you can say something three or four times and it will still get miscommunicated. I had someone call the hospital back to tell Levi's doctor, "Don't do any more surgeries on Levi. We're pulling him out of the country."

We told the doctor this several times, but I still wasn't sure she understood us. Moments like these are somewhat common in our daily existence in China. In fact, we call them *China Moments*—times when you cannot seem to convey a simple instruction or idea because of the language barrier. Trying to tell the doctor not to amputate any more of Levi was similar to the scene in the movie *Monty Python and the Holy Grail* when the king is trying to instruct the guards not to let his son, the prince, leave the castle until he returns. Their conversation went something like this:

King: Do not release the prince until I return.

Guard: Okay, so before you get here, I'll let the prince leave.

King: No, wait until I return. Then you can let the prince leave.

Guard: Right, so I'll leave, and when I return, I'll let the prince go.

King: No, make sure you hold the prince until I leave. Don't release him to anyone but me.

Guard: So if you don't return, I'll let him leave before you get back.

And on and on it goes.

With no time to spare, all I could do was pray, *Dear God, please don't let the doctors take any more of Levi's limbs.* I scrambled to prepare for our trip to Boston, which was scheduled for early the next day. I hadn't admitted to Cynthia how afraid I actually was at the prospect of traveling alone to Boston with Levi. Truth be told, I had never recovered from the trauma I had gone through during 9/11. During that crisis, I had been separated from my family while traveling from California to Washington D.C.

Ever since that experience, I never wanted to travel alone again. Now, faced with the prospect of having to board a plane with a sick infant and fly more than ten thousand miles into another uncertain future, anxiety began to overtake me. *God, I don't want to travel to Boston alone,* I prayed. But how could I possibly ask United Airlines for one more thing? *I know I don't deserve this request,* I continued in my prayer, *and this would be icing on the cake, but please, do not make me go alone.* They had already provided the "miracle" we needed for Levi. Was it wrong to ask for more?

I finally got up the nerve to call Cynthia again. When I heard her voice at the other end of the line, I said, "Cynthia, I know you have gone above and beyond the call of duty in getting tickets for Levi and me to get to Boston. But is there any way I could get a ticket so that my daughter, Emily, could come with me, too? I will need a helper, and I would be so grateful for her support." Emily would buffer the pain of being away from the entire family for whatever time period we needed to be gone. To my amazement, Cynthia cheerfully agreed to help, and she was able to quickly get approval for Emily's ticket.

Now one more transportation detail needed to be worked out: How was I to get Levi from the hospital to the airport safely?

Again, God was working out the details through compassionate friends. I called Nancy Fraser to let her know the good news. She spent the evening gathering up items for our trip— a baby bag, blankets, bottles, diapers—everything I would need for Levi while he was away. Nancy also called her friend, Roberta Lipson, who had founded the Beijing United Family Hospital, to ask if the hospital would be willing to provide the ambulance transportation for Levi from the Beijing Children's Hospital to the airport the next day. Roberta said yes without hesitation.

I had awakened the day before to grim news about Levi. Now, with passport and plane tickets in hand, I was going to bed that night with nothing but hope for that little boy. If I could just get him to Boston, I would know I had done the best I could for him. We weren't there yet, and Boston remained a distant hope. I still had miles to go before I could sleep.

CHAPTER SIX

Bind and Unite

Jesus looked at them and said,
"With men it is impossible, but not with God;
for with God all things are possible."
—MARK 10:27 (NKJV)

救

STATESIDE, MY FRIEND TRACI NELSON was busy. She's a home-schooling mom I had met in Vancouver, Washington, while John was an attorney there. I called myself and my friends "buck-wheat." We were into wholesome eating and talking about budgets and immunizations. Traci was a woman who showed me how to live authentically. Though she walked quietly and gently through life, she carried a big stick when it came to her faith. She and I had been corresponding by e-mail about Levi's needs since the day we received him, and with every new prayer request, Traci quietly prayed. Every request she made—both big and small—was answered in heroic ways.

For instance, it turned out United Airlines had scheduled us to arrive in Boston just in time for the annual Boston Marathon, when extremely scarce hotel rooms were costing an arm and a leg. Even my mom, who is in the travel business, had no success finding us accommodations. Traci also spent countless hours making phone calls and pleading with different businesses for help. I was in awe when I got her e-mail the day before our trip. Excitedly she said, "Lisa, Holiday Inn Select has a room available for you, and it's only one block away from Shriners Hospitals for Children. Also, Thrifty Car Rental has a car for you. And guess what?" she added, barely able to contain herself, "Everything is free!"

I like a great deal as much as anyone, but getting these details worked out—and at no charge—was beyond my wildest imagination. We were living from day to day, never knowing for sure if or how we'd be able to pay our rent each month. It's stressful enough trying to save someone's life. Doing it on a shoestring—and a broken one at that—forces you to depend on God like nothing else. The good thing is you get to see His generosity every day. Each time there's food on the table, it's like a gift from heaven. John had always aspired to this kind of lifestyle. He was an officer in the army during the Persian Gulf War and was among the first troops deployed. During this time, he read the famous biography of missionary George Mueller. Mueller had helped thousands of orphans, yet he never knew where the money to sustain his work would come from. He prayed, and milk would miraculously show up at his door right before he needed it. He lived his whole life by faith. John was taken by Mueller's "living by faith" approach, so he decided to start applying this same concept to all aspects of our lives.

Receiving plane tickets, a hotel room, a rental car—it was all milk on the doorstep. And that wasn't even the end of Traci's news.

"Lisa, I have chills," she wrote in an e-mail. "Do you know what the name Levi means?"

"No," I said. "I named him after your son, Levi, just because I thought it was a cool name."

"Lisa," Traci continued excitedly, "Levi means 'to bind and unite.'"

From the day we received Levi, he had done nothing but bring people together from all over the world. Through prayers, financial assistance, and media attention, our little Levi was bridging the lives of people who otherwise would have no way to be joined together. I was starting to catch a glimpse of how Jesus' mother must have felt watching her Son grow up. Even as an infant, He had caught the attention of everyone from lowly shepherds to King Herod. Everyone wanted to see Him and no one remained the same after an encounter with Him. This was a little like the way it was starting to seem with Levi.

救

Traci's phone call came on the heels of a huge media opportunity we had been given the previous day. If ever Levi bound and united people, it was during our interview with *China Youth*

Daily, a popular newspaper with a circulation in the millions. Melody Zhang is a warm, savvy professional woman who runs Children's Hope International (CHI), a major international adoption agency in Beijing, and she had arranged for us to meet with a team of reporters at the hospital. The newspaper is owned by the Communist party and they came to report on Levi's story.

CHI paid for Levi's first surgery at the Beijing Children's Hospital. They are committed to helping as many orphans get adopted as possible. Levi's was a surgery about which someone easily could have said, "You know, this baby is probably going to die. Why spend the money on this when we could use it to help other kids who have a better chance?" Instead, CHI saw the extreme need and said, "We're going to do the surgery." Having no means of our own to pay for his medical treatment, we knew this was no small favor.

Just before we were set to do this interview, our son Oliver, who was three at the time, fell at home and cut open his forehead. We didn't have health insurance, and I couldn't afford the foreign hospital, so we had to rush him to the local Langfang hospital, the same place that first had cared for Levi. When it came time for them to stitch up Oliver, they told me to step outside the room. When I heard Oliver's cries, I realized they hadn't given him anything for the pain, but it was too late to rush in and stop them. This reminded me of Levi and the chronic, searing pain he had been in for weeks now. I was grateful I could be present for Oliver in his pain. For Levi, we were trying to do the best we could for him, but the reality was he needed a mommy to soothe and comfort him.

Fortunately, Oliver rebounded from the trauma quickly, and we raced to Beijing and got to the hospital just in time to conduct the Chinese newspaper interview. The reporters were intrigued by the fact that Americans had given up their prosperous lives in the United States to come and help special needs orphans—the least of the least—in China. This coverage gave Levi and the children's village at Langfang exposure throughout all of China, which helped bring about some surprising new relationships for us down the road. Our interview with *China Youth Daily* would be the first of many more media spotlights on Levi. At this moment, though, I was more concerned about nailing down the details of our trip to Boston—and finding a caregiver for Levi.

救

The next day, I said my good-byes to the rest of our boys before leaving home. John, Emily, and I arrived at the Beijing Hospital early in the morning. After signing release papers, I heard these parting words from the doctor: "If he starts to leak body fluids, you're in trouble."

Nancy Fraser was waiting for us at the hospital to help us check Levi out. Nancy accompanied us out of the hospital. Handing me a baby bag bursting with supplies, she said, "I have friends in Boston who might be able to help you while you're there." she didn't have time to give me their names or contact information, but somehow just knowing there was a connection between our China friend and some people from Boston made the world feel smaller to me.

John and I embraced. I could have stayed in that moment forever, feeling safe and secure. What awaited me next was a whirlwind of uncertainties. Reluctantly, I kissed John good-bye.

Emily and I loaded ourselves into the ambulance after Levi was situated, and we rode with him to the airport. When we got there, we discovered that United Airlines had generously upgraded Levi, Emily, and me to business class.

Knowing we were traveling with such a sick child, United had us wait in the corporate lounge until it was time for our flight. Xuan Fu, a businesswoman from Chicago who was also waiting in the lounge, saw Levi. Levi no longer was dressed from head to toe in gauze. Immediately, streams of tears rolled down her face. It was amazing to see her compassion.

"What happened to this baby?" she asked. I told her Levi's story, and as I did, tears repeatedly welled up in her eyes. I knew seeing Levi had affected her in a life-changing way.

Just before our flight was preparing to board, I saw a familiar face. "Danny, what are you doing on this flight?" I asked in disbelief. Danny Coyle was the son of one of our team members. His grandmother had just died and he was heading home for the funeral. At the ticket counter I asked if they would be willing to let Danny have a seat next to us. United Airlines agreed to it, which was a huge help. Danny assisted me on the plane when I was physically exhausted and needed help taking care of Levi. God seemed to be surrounding us with everyone we needed to make the journey safely.

Finally, we boarded the plane and prepared for takeoff. The flight attendants insisted I pick up Levi and hold him upright in case there were any sudden, unexpected movements of the plane. He had been flat on his back for the last three weeks following surgery in Beijing, and to be honest, I was scared to hold him. The Beijing doctor's warning about leaking body fluids haunted me.

With no medical training, I had no idea what I would do if this scenario played out. I also had noticed that his eyes kept rolling back in his head. I wondered if, on top of all his physical problems, he had a mental problem too.

Thankfully, everything went smoothly on takeoff. Flight attendants showed us uncommon care and attention throughout our flight. Xuan Fu, the businesswoman I met in United's lounge, ended up on our same flight. Over and over, she came to our row to see if I needed anything or if there was anything she could do to help. Between one of her trips to the front of the plane, a surprise visitor appeared from a few rows behind us. "I know you!" a woman I had never met said warmly. It turned out it was Roberta Lipson, the founder of the United Family Hospital in Beijing. I was so glad I had the chance to thank her in person for providing the ambulance ride earlier that day. Roberta and I hit it off right away. She was a no-nonsense professional woman, but we related to each other as fellow Jewish women. During the flight she repeatedly visited Emily and me to see if there was anything she could do to help.

The flight went smoothly except for one small hitch. After about 20 hours of travel, Emily and I were exhausted. She had had it with the matching mother-daughter Chinese outfits we were wearing. She got up to use the bathroom, and when she came back, she had decided not to fuss with the ties that held the outfit together. To her surprise (and everyone's on the airplane), her bottoms had completely fallen off. My eight-year-old daughter was walking in her underwear—providing much-needed comedic relief. It was a rare, light moment because next, when I looked down at Levi, I noticed he had green fluids leaking from his bandages. I must have ruptured Levi's wounds when I had lifted him hours before.

God, I asked fearfully, *am I killing this baby?*

The doctor's ominous words as we left Beijing hung over me like the darkness shrouding Chicago at twilight as we landed for a brief layover. I was anxious to check Levi's wounds. Xuan Fu followed us as far as security would let her go. Before we parted, she asked, "Lisa, how much money do you have with you?" At that moment I realized I had left town with only $50 in my purse. I told her how much money I had in my wallet, and she slipped $100 into my hand, and gave me a phone card to use to let John know we had made it safely. I later learned in an e-mail from a coworker of Xuan Fu's that nothing had touched her more than meeting Levi.

In the short time we had in between flights, I quickly found a quiet place to lay Levi down on his blanket to examine his wounds. I considered trying to rewrap the dressings as best I could, but I worried that undoing them would only make matters worse. His eyes were rolling back in his head continually now. Would he die in my arms?

Time was working against us. Exhausted and fearful, Emily and I boarded another plane for the last leg of our trip—Chicago to Boston. Again, the United flight attendants took special care of us. One flight attendant came up to me toward the end of the flight and said, "Lisa, I don't have a lot of money. I don't make a lot of money. Here's $20." I could not believe the outpouring of compassion being showered on us.

Levi was having that effect on a lot of people. It was as though God were presenting him to humanity and asking the question: "Now, what will you do with this child who is hurting?" From where I sat, compassion for Levi was overflowing like a cold drink of water in a Biggie-size cup.

救

Landing in Boston at 11 P.M. was surreal. A media circus awaited us when we got off the plane. Apparently, Traci Nelson's prayers netted more than just a few nights' stay in the city. She had tipped off the local TV stations about our story. After our newspaper coverage in China, we were now facing television news crews from Boston affiliates for ABC and Fox. They featured our journey from Beijing to Boston with our little burned baby. Everywhere we went, we found people who seemed intrigued by Levi's story.

As exhausted as we were, I revived instantly when I saw the sudden rush of excitement at our arrival. In the glare of flashing emergency lights, Emily and I loaded Levi and all our luggage into the ambulance and rushed from the airport to Shriners Hospitals for Children. A team of doctors awaited our arrival outside of Shriners, including Dr. John Schulz. "We've been waiting for this baby," he said. I could have collapsed in tears at that moment.

Here we were, finally meeting face to face with the doctor, a stranger, who was willing to save Levi's life. It should have taken six to nine months to get Levi to Boston. Instead, with God's help and all the others who had banded together to save Levi, it had taken us only six weeks! Immediately, medical personnel rushed Levi into the emergency room. I left Emily and our luggage with the ambulance driver and followed Levi's gurney.

Dr. Rob Sheridan, who did many of the subsequent surgeries on Levi, evaluated him and explained that there are four phases of care for burn victims: initial evaluation, resuscitation, definitive wound closure, and rehabilitation and reconstruction. "We're getting Levi somewhere between wound closure and rehabilitation and reconstruction," he said. "The younger burn victims are, the more staging is involved in their rehabilitation and reconstruction. Infants quickly outgrow their results, so they need to be able to return over the years for repeated surgeries."

I asked about Levi's eyes rolling back in his head. "Imagine burning yourself and how agonizing this is," Dr. Sheridan said. "Now, imagine this same pain over your entire body. That's what Levi is feeling." He was in such prolonged, intense pain that his little body was going into shock. In China he had been given only acetaminophen, even after his amputations. The doctor explained that phantom pains are intense. Phantom pain is when your nerve endings think your limb is still attached try to send pain signals to it. It was almost unbelievable he had endured the pain for so long without shutting down completely.

While the doctors conducted their evaluation of Levi and cleaned up the wounds that had ruptured during our flight, I went to find Emily in the waiting room. When I came out to see how she was doing, she jumped out of her seat. "Mommy, look what the ambulance driver gave us!" Emily held up four dollars and handed me an envelope. On it was written "May God bless you." When I opened it, I discovered $40 tucked inside. Another jug of milk on the doorstep.

CHAPTER SEVEN

Turning in My Keys for Heaven

I've been painting pictures of Egypt,
Leaving out what it lacks
The future feels so hard,
And I want to go back!
But the places that used to fit me,
Cannot hold the things I've learned
Those roads were closed off to me
While my back was turned.

—SARA GROVES, FROM "PAINTING PICTURES OF EGYPT"*

EVEN THOUGH BOSTON IS not my hometown, landing there and getting settled at the hospital felt like coming home from college at Thanksgiving. Everyone was waiting expectantly for our

---

arrival, all of the familiar sights and sounds of America greeted us, everyone doted over us like a mother does her travel-weary child—it was as if my whole body intuitively knew it was home. Just being able to read the street signs was a welcome treat. For the first time in weeks, I felt myself relax.

The level of medical care at Shriners Hospitals also brought me hope. Before they even allowed me to enter Levi's room, the nurses instructed me to scrub up and put on a gown and mask. I was shocked when I saw his new surroundings. He looked like the character in the TV movie *The Boy in the Plastic Bubble,* lying in a germ-free tent in a private, brightly painted room.

Levi had several nurses tending to his every need, and all of the nurses wore protective gloves when they handled him. *It's good to be back in the United States.* The staff's response to Levi's pain was immediate. Recognizing the shock his body had gone into by the way his eyes were rolling back in his head, they quickly administered morphine. For the first time in nearly a month, Levi settled into a comfortable sleep—his first pain-free rest since his accident weeks before. Between the quiet of his slumber and the ease of being able to communicate clearly in English, I felt like I was in paradise. *Who would have thought that the girl who freaked out over germs would actually be comparing a hospital room to paradise?* I smiled inside as I sipped a cold complimentary cranberry juice from the room's minirefrigerator.

The hospital had set up a bed in the corner of Levi's room for Emily and me to take turns resting in. Because there were two of us, we couldn't spend the night there, but it was a wonderful change of pace from the hardback seat I had spent hours sitting in at the Beijing Children's Hospital.

After getting Levi stabilized the first night, the doctors scheduled him for a round of skin grafts. Levi's body had rejected much of the donor skin that had been grafted in Beijing. Dr. Sheridan explained to me that skin grafts are done by harvesting any available healthy skin. On infants, the task is delicate and tedious because their skin is extremely thin, like an old person's. "You have to be so careful to harvest skin in tissue-thin layers so that you're not creating unnecessary scar tissue," he said. "On Levi, there is very little skin to harvest. Pretty much anything that hasn't been burned will be fair game." The doctors began what would be a series of multiple painstaking surgeries on his face, hand, knee, and torso. They were impressed with the work the Beijing surgeons had done on his left arm. Though it had required two amputations, the arm was now healing well and required no additional surgery.

By noon, both Emily and I were feeling the full effects of jet lag. With a 13-hour time difference, our internal clocks thought it was about 2 A.M. We headed back to our hotel for a short nap to try to reprogram our body clocks. After a brief sleep, I was awakened by the phone's ringing.

"Is this Lisa Bentley?" the woman on the other end asked.

"Yes, it is."

The caller explained that she had seen Emily and me on the news the night before when we had first arrived in Boston. She and her husband were from Canada and staying in our hotel. "Would you like to meet for dinner? We're in the process of adopting our first child from China, and we'd love to be able to talk to you."

That evening we told each other about our lives, and then they asked us if we wanted to go with them to Park Street Church for Sunday service the next day. Park Street Church is located in the middle of Boston on the Freedom Trail. Its historic white steeple stands in stark contrast to the newer, modern architecture that defines Boston. We agreed to go with them, but the next day jet lag had set in, so I decided to take Emily to an earlier service on our own. Weaving through the maze of traffic and people, I could see the steeple of Park Street Church, but I couldn't figure out how to get to it. The streets were a sea of people—joggers, T-shirt vendors, and cars crowded everywhere. Finally, exasperated from being lost, I pulled over to a corner, rolled down my window and spoke to the first couple who caught my eye. "Hi," I said. "I'm visiting from China, and I'm trying to find Park Street Church."

The couple immediately asked, "Are you Lisa Bentley?"

I said, "Yes."

They responded, "We're Nancy Fraser's friends!"

My mouth dropped open. John always tells me that serendipity follows me wherever I go, but this was outrageous. Here were Kim and Kyu Lee, the friends Nancy had mentioned in passing as I was hurriedly getting ready to load into the ambulance in Beijing. It turns out these friends of hers were both pediatric doctors, and they just happened to be standing on the very street corner where I decided to pull over to ask for directions.

I couldn't have arranged this if I tried. It was an unexpected blessing to me on Boston Marathon Sunday—meeting two more links on a chain that was now being forged across continents. After finding a place to park the car, Emily and I met up with Kim and Kyu and spent a few minutes chatting before church. They asked if they could look in on Levi periodically while he was at Shriners. What a godsend to have two pediatricians keeping an eye on our little guy. We exchanged contact information with a vow to meet again next time we were in Boston.

After church Emily and I walked through Boston Public Garden and discovered the bronze duckling statues from Robert McCloskey's book, *Make Way for Ducklings*. Just blocks away, Levi was in surgery. No one sends a child into an operating room without some degree of apprehension, and yet in the beauty of that spring afternoon, I rested in the knowledge that we had done the best we could for him. Our long journey had finally come to an end; we had done our part. We didn't know for sure if he would survive, but he was finally right where he needed to be. Together, Emily and I celebrated this victory as we floated on a swan boat across the lake in the middle of the park.

救

How does a mother pick a substitute to care for her child in her absence?

This was the question that nagged at my thoughts even

before I left for Boston. *Is this what the mothers of Chinese babies thought about before deciding to leave their children at our gate?* I knew most mothers intentionally selected the orphanage we worked at because of our reputation for taking in special-needs orphans. When parents leave a baby outside our orphanage, they know they are delivering their child to a place of safety. We are their baby's only hope for survival. Likewise, I knew I had delivered Levi to a place of healing and hope. Unlike most of the parents who leave their babies on our doorstep, I would get to see Levi again. It would just be a matter of time.

I had continued letting my calls go to voicemail at the hotel because I wanted to focus all my attention on Levi's medical needs at the hospital. With only one day left before we needed to leave Boston, I realized I might have been procrastinating about choosing a caregiver partly out of fear. *Who will I be able to find to take care of Levi?* It wasn't that I considered myself the only mother capable of caring for Levi. Given all he had been through, though, I wanted to be sure I placed him in the best possible hands, with someone who was willing to watch over him and pray by his side. He would be in intensive care for at least another two months, possibly longer.

Just as my anxiety level started to escalate, the phone rang. This time I decided to take the call. To my surprise, it was Lisa Scott, my former pastor's wife from the church we attended in Maryland when John had served as a JAG, or military attorney. The Scotts had been supportive of our work in China, and they were following Levi's story closely. She said, "Lisa, I think I've found a good match for you for a caregiver for Levi. Could you call Linda Evans? She used to go to our church in Maryland, but now she lives in Boston."

Grateful for the lead, I dialed Linda's number. After chatting for a few minutes, I knew from the kind tone of her voice that Linda had the warmth and compassion I was looking for, plus she already was driving into Boston several times a week to take her teenage daughter, Rachel, to her ice skating lessons. Logistically, visiting Levi worked with her daily schedule. As soon as Linda learned that Emily and I needed to leave the next day, she and her husband, Don, drove from Plymouth to Boston to meet us right away.

I was impressed that these complete strangers were willing to drive more than an hour to meet me and find out how they could help Levi. I don't know how Levi managed to do it. For weeks all he had done was lie there, and yet in that time he had mysteriously bound total strangers together, uniting us in a fight to save his life. *What was it about him that made everyone want to drop what they were doing and help?* Prayers of gratitude flowed from my heart as Emily and I walked down the street to Shriners to wait for Linda and Don to arrive.

When Linda and Don made their way to Levi's room, they found me keeping watch by his bed in a chair, and Emily asleep on the bed in the corner. They washed their hands, donned their gowns and masks, and the three of us stood talking. "Linda, do you want to hold Levi?" I asked. Even though Levi had freshly dressed wounds and IV tubes were attached to different parts of his body, the nurses had given us the green light to hold him. Linda and Don both adore babies, so holding

Levi came as naturally to them as if they were rocking one of their own.

While Linda cradled him, a nurse stepped into the room. "Would it be all right if I changed Levi's bandages while he's on your lap?" she asked Linda.

Linda agreed to do this, but afterward she confessed, "I can't believe I just did that without getting sick." In the past she had always been too squeamish to watch her own kids get shots or stitches.

I clicked right away with Linda and Don. When I shared Levi's whole harrowing story up to that point, Linda said without hesitation, "I'd like to be his caregiver while you're in China." With peace in my heart for having found this guardian angel, I gave them authorization to visit Levi after we left, as well as Kim and Kyu Lee, but the hospital still would need to contact me for verbal authorizations for any additional surgeries. Emily and I stayed with Levi in his room until midnight that night, savoring the hours we had to hold him, to finally comfort him the way I had longed to from the first time I met him. To rock him, sing to him, pray over him—these were tender mercies that filled my mother's heart. Parting definitely would be a sweet sorrow.

I had mixed emotions about leaving when I woke up the next day. On the one hand, I felt like I had run the race for Levi's life. Getting him to Shriners was like finishing my first Boston Marathon. I knew I was leaving him in the best care possible. On the other hand, after meeting with Dr. Schulz that morning, his prognosis was still uncertain. Blood infection remained an ever-present threat. There were no guarantees we would ever see Levi alive again. With a heavy heart, I said a bittersweet good-bye to our peacefully sleeping baby as I left him at Shriners' gate.

救

Getting Levi to Boston also marked the approximate end of our three-month visit to China. After falling in love with Levi, the thought of leaving China seemed foreign to me. Then again, being back on U.S. soil reminded me how much I loved my native country. When Emily and I left Shriners, we headed for California where we would be meeting up with John and the other kids to visit family. Then we were on to Vancouver, Washington, to tie up the loose ends of our life.

While we were in California visiting family, we needed a place to stay. Saddleback Church, the megachurch led by Rick Warren, author of *The Purpose-Driven Life*, offered us the use of one of their homes reserved for missionaries on furlough. When Kay Warren learned we were orphan relief workers from China who also were in need of a car, she brought over her son's vehicle for us to use. Kay and I talked for about 10 minutes, in which time I was able to briefly share about Levi. I could tell by the tears in her eyes that she was touched by his story.

Later that day, we drove into an upscale area to do some banking. When we pulled up at the bank in the Warrens' beatup old car, a woman standing nearby looked at us, counted the kids, and handed me a $20 bill. When I got home, I told John what happened. Far from being offended, he was happy—we got $20! Things like that never happened when we drove the sports car, which was now collecting dust in our old garage.

After spending a few days in California, we headed north to Vancouver. We hadn't been able to sell our house before moving to China because there was a glut of houses on the market at the time. Thankfully, we had found renters to live there while we had been away for the past three months. Seeing the remains of our old life, I remembered the comfortable existence we had left behind. Before China, John had earned a good living as an attorney. Now, we earned our living by raising support through donations from family and friends. Our first family newsletter, which is the means most relief workers use to raise funds to remain on the field, garnered us only $350.

With such meager funding, it quickly became evident we would have no way to continue making our payments. Subsequent appeals for donations had netted us enough funding to squeak by the last two months in China. The fact that the cost of living is so much lower there helped matters a lot. But still, providing for so many kids takes a substantial amount of money no matter how much rice you eat. Life in China would be no picnic.

Now that Levi had come into our lives, we were at a crossroads. Would we come back to America where John could get a job as an attorney again and save the house and car? We had never been late or missed a payment in our entire married life. John took his role as provider seriously, and the thought of being negligent financially was an intense struggle for him. But coming back to America to salvage the life we had built here would mean letting go of Levi. How could we abandon him again?

There I stood with all the keys to my life—a house key and two car keys in one hand; Levi and a life in China in the other. Door number one or door number two. *Come on, Lisa, what's it gonna be?*

With peace in my heart, I chose China. Though a life in China would mean having little materially, I knew I would possess everything there. I wouldn't have a 401(k), but I would wake up to milk on the doorstep each morning.

Leaving Vancouver this time, I felt like I had once and for all turned in my keys and all sense of ownership of my life. For a short time, we continued to rent out the house, but ultimately the house and cars were repossessed. We headed back to China with our old life gone and a new life ahead of us.

CHAPTER EIGHT

Angels All Around

Like weather, one's fortune may change by the evening.
—LUU MENGZHENG, SONG DYNASTY

救

AS WE SKIMMED THROUGH THE smog on our approach into Beijing, I pondered the work that lay ahead of us. How would I balance the needs of my family, the work that needed to get done with the orphans, and the long-distance care of Levi? Levi was in good hands at Shriners, and yet we still had about 25 other babies who needed medical attention at the children's village in Langfang, not to mention my need to buckle down and create some stability in our home. In some ways, I was relieved to not have to deal with the intense day-to-day drama of caring for Levi. That task now fell on Linda and Don Evans.

The day after Emily and I left Boston, Linda returned to

Shriners to start her tenure as Levi's caregiver. Even though tubes, bloody bandages, and raw wounds shrouded Levi's body, Linda spent hours holding him and pouring her love into him. Within days the hospital staff was able to move Levi out of isolation—no more "bubble boy"—and into a regular room. What we hadn't expected or hoped for was all the extra love and attention the entire nursing staff would give to Levi. Like mother hens, they instinctively wanted to make him part of their family.

Any time he squeaked, all the nurses wanted to hold him. "No, it's my turn," they would argue. It was as if they couldn't bear the thought of his being an orphan, so instead they treated him like the Emperor of Shriners. He became their prized possession. Maybe it was his mahogany eyes, which were round as saucers. Looking at Levi was like deep calling out to deep. Something in his eyes beckoned your soul.

Whatever the attraction, the most important task facing him now was drinking enough fluids to recover from the multiple surgeries he had endured. After the skin grafts, it was critical that he stay hydrated to give the newly harvested tissue a way to take hold and heal. Linda or Don continued to visit Levi nearly every day, driving an hour each way. They or the doctors gave me regular updates on Levi's progress or any problems he was encountering. Whenever he needed to undergo more surgery, his doctors always contacted me to get my verbal authorization.

Even with so much communication, as time went on, I started feeling a little left out. On Mother's Day I called the hospital and discovered Linda was in the room visiting Levi. *How lucky she is to celebrate this day with him!* I was grateful for the loving care Levi was receiving, but a tiny part of me felt jealous too. *I want to be his mommy!* my heart cried.

Almost from the start, I knew I was supposed to be Levi's mother. But John and I had broached the subject of adopting Levi only in passing. With my love growing each day for this child, however, the time had come to make a plan. Complicating everything was the fact that John had his eye on another orphan who had captured his heart from the first time he had met her. Miao Miao was one of the first babies to live at one of our foster homes in Langfang. She had come to us after being abandoned in a train station in Tianjin, a major city one hour's drive southeast of Langfang. Most likely her parents were poor villagers who did not have the money to pay for her medical care.

After taking Miao Miao in, we got her the surgery to correct her spina bifida. Then we waited confidently for a family to adopt her. As Valentine's Day approached and I asked John what he wanted for a gift, he answered without hesitation, "What I really want is for us to adopt Miao Miao." We both knew this was a foolish decision because at that time we had four biological kids of our own, no money, no health insurance—and no sports car. Yet I knew Miao Miao had been placed on John's heart like a baby at the gate asking, *What will you do with me now that you've found me?* I thought Miao Miao was charming, but I didn't feel that instantaneous welling up of natural love toward her as I did with Levi. For me, loving her as my own child would be a decision, not an emotional reaction.

Every adoptive parent wonders if there will be a natural attraction to a new child. And what if there's not? Does that mean you love the child less or are incapable of really loving him or her? No. You must simply love in deed first, and the feelings of love will follow. Our society has this love thing all twisted around. We think the basis of love is our feelings, but it's not. The New Testament teaches that love is a decision to act. Love is always about what you *do* for others, not what you *feel*.

Unfortunately for us, even after we had resolved the debate over whether or not to adopt Miao Miao, we discovered that a wonderful family already had been selected to adopt her. Now thinking the door to adopt her had closed, we let go of our desire to make her our daughter and simply waited with her while the details of her adoption became final. This also freed us to pursue adopting Levi, though John still wanted to take this slowly. He wanted to give me time to see if the love I felt for Levi was a flash of emotion or the beginning of a deep-rooted, enduring love.

救

From the minute we returned to China without Levi, we hit the ground running. First, we needed to pack everything up to move into our new home. We didn't shed any tears when we said good-bye to the house of jumping rats. Now, knowing we were going to stay in China, I focused on feathering our new nest, helping the kids catch up on the schoolwork we hadn't done during the year, cooking meals, and exploring our surroundings. John had taken on a full-time leadership role at the orphanage. Finally fulfilling his dream of serving orphans in China, John began to thrive and grow in a way I had never seen him do before.

As summer wore on, I enjoyed China more and more. But with Levi gone, our family felt incomplete. He had been the focal point of everything I did during our first few months in China.

By mid-July he had gained a healthy amount of weight and was ready to be discharged from Shriners Hospitals for Children, but he still needed to stay in the Boston area for ongoing outpatient treatment. Linda willingly offered to take in her "boyfriend," as she fondly referred to Levi, for the remaining time he would need follow-up treatment.

Finally, about three weeks later, the time had come for us to retrieve him from Boston. Once again, United Airlines generously offered to sponsor Levi's return flight to China. He still had a clinic visit scheduled before he was ready to be released for travel back to China, so I headed for Boston with Emily, planning to spend a few nights at the Evans's home.

When I saw Levi again for the first time, I could not believe how plump and cheerful he was. His facial skin grafts had healed beautifully, and his smile lit up his whole face. We had a wonderful time reuniting after three months. The "wonderful" part, however, faded during our first night together. Linda had given me her bed next to Levi in the lower level. "He's your baby," she said smiling. Her cheerful willingness to give up her station should have tipped me off.

Levi woke up crying every hour of the night. He had developed what I call "arms disease." If he didn't have his needs catered to immediately, that boy would scream at such a decibel, it felt as if my eardrums might burst. I quickly realized there was no way I could sustain the level of caregiving Linda and the Shriners nurses had provided. The next morning, exhausted and crabby, I said, "Linda, you're going to notice Levi crying a lot more." It would take some time, but I needed to start instilling better sleep habits—for both his sake and mine!

When it came time for us to drive to the airport and say our good-byes to the Evanses, Linda could barely hold back the tears. Bound now by her love for this little orphan, Linda and the rest of her family were inextricably linked to Levi. Their compassion and service were like adding reinforced steel to the heavy-gauge chain that had formed around Levi's life.

At the same time, little Miao Miao's pending adoption had fallen through. For reasons known only to the Chinese ministry that handles placing orphans in families, she would need to wait a little longer for her forever family, and we needed to decide if we would be Levi's.

Job number one once we returned to China was training Levi to sleep through the night. We brought him to live in our own house to be sure he was getting the follow-up medical care the

Shriners' doctors had instructed us to give him. This included hours of massage and movement each day to ensure that the scar tissue didn't harden.

If Levi were going to become part of our lives, we would all need to start treating him like a regular member of the family, in spite of his physical needs. It took awhile to get used to having a baby in the house, especially one with so many needs, but gradually we all grew accustomed to our new routine with Levi.

For about six months, we marked time by entries in his baby book. Then the bleeding started. Watching Levi grow was pure joy, but it also carried a curse. As he grew, his scars needed to be reopened to allow for bone growth. His wounds splitting open signaled the need for more surgery. Leaving China would mean cutting through massive red tape again, so John started working feverishly toward this goal. Even though we had been through this process before, this time he was hitting some major roadblocks. For instance, every time he tried to fax citizen services at the U.S. embassy to get an expedited visa based on medical necessity, the document wouldn't go through. When he tried to call, he got answering machines and no one would return his calls. It was like trying to call the White House to get help. It just wasn't happening. Finally, in complete frustration, he prayed, "God, I just can't do it anymore. I'm ready to explode. I know You want this little boy to get the surgery he needs, but I can't make it happen. If this is going to happen, then You are going to have to do it."

The next morning the phone rang before John had even

gotten out of bed. "Are you the caretaker for Levi?" the voice on the other end asked.

"Yes," John responded.

"Would you be able to meet at the American consulate at 10:30 this morning? You have a specially set appointment with the consul general himself."

"Yes," John said, "we'll be there."

John found out that our friends John and Dinah Watkins from the Beijing International Christian Fellowship had taken an interest in Levi. That concern led John Watkins, a well-respected businessman in Beijing, to call the consul general on our behalf.

When John and I met with the consul general, he wanted to find out what our needs were. After learning what we were trying to do—get Levi back to Boston—he took action to push everything aside that was hindering us from helping Levi. He granted us a visa on the spot, and gave us his business card, telling us to call him anytime in the future when Levi needed to get to the States.

From his office, we went over to United Airlines where they gave us two free business-class tickets and reduced-priced tickets for the children. The situation went from a dead stop with John calling out to God for help to our entire family being on an airplane bound for the States within 30 hours. It was too much to conceive of—a miracle of sorts—and more was yet to come.

When we took off for Boston, we had $2,000. Two organizations, Life Outreach International and the International

Community for Chinese Orphans, had each given us $1,000 to cover expenses for the trip. We were deeply grateful, but we knew it wasn't going to be enough to cover our expenses for a six-week stay in Boston. The timing of this surgery came at a particularly hard time for our family—we were tired and a bit worn out. Nonetheless, we left China with the faith that God would some way, somehow provide for our needs.

God acted sooner than we imagined He would. That United Airlines flight became the venue for a revival meeting of sorts. A constant stream of people kept coming up to our family to meet us and find out about Levi. Once one person heard his story, another one would come up and want to talk with us. Poor John. He had never flown business class and he was trying so hard to enjoy his filet mignon! But he met everyone from the pilot to a friend of Roberta Lipson.

Meeting that friend, Norman Kaplan, will forever be etched in our memory. He was walking down the aisle past our seats when the sight of Levi stopped him cold. This wealthy business owner in Beijing began asking us questions about Levi, our family, and our work. During that conversation, while John's filet was growing cold, we learned that Norman went to synagogue with Roberta. At the end our conversation, Norman took out his checkbook. He had only one check left, which he had started to make out to someone else for $75. Norman crossed out the other person's name, changed the amount to $3,750, and handed it to us.

About 20 minutes later, Ron Martin, an executive from Caterpillar Inc., came over to talk to us. When we finished, he handed us a check for $1,000. By the time our plane touched down in the United States, God had already provided $4,750 through the generosity of our new friends.

But that wasn't all. In Boston, the Holiday Inn Select, which was right next to Shriners let us have a suite for our entire stay at no charge. Next, four churches asked John to speak, and those opportunities provided more income. By the time we returned to Beijing, God had left just enough milk on our doorstep to pay for our entire six-week trip.

John's last speaking engagement was for a Sunday evening service in Maryland. We had an early-morning flight from Boston back to Beijing on Tuesday morning. We needed to leave Maryland at 9 P.M. and arrive in Boston early enough to get Levi released and retrieve our luggage from Kim and Kyu Lee's house where we had been storing everything. It dawned on us that we had a major logistical problem. We had too much luggage and too many kids to fit in the minivan. It was physically impossible for John to get the luggage to the airport and checked through the security system all in one trip.

John and I prayed, "God, we need your help. We can't do this by ourselves."

Thirty minutes later, the phone rang. It was a woman named Sandra Suzio who had attended a Baptist convention in Boston that weekend. She had purchased several tapes to listen to on the car ride home, and one she popped in featured Kay Warren as the speaker. Little did I know that our brief exchange the day she came to drop off her son's car during our stay in California would become material for her women's conferences. She had been so moved by Levi's story, which I had shared with her in 10 minutes or less, that she now retold it at some of the conferences she attended as a speaker.

As Sandra Suzio listened to Kay Warren tell the story of Levi, she, too, was moved by his plight. She suddenly felt compelled to see how she could help us. Without knowing whether we were in the United States or in China, Sandra called Saddleback Church in California to find out how to reach us. Through the help of Bucky Rosenbaum, who was on staff there at the time, she tracked us down to the house where we were staying in Maryland.

Much to our amazement, Sandra said she would take care of everything. When we finally arrived in Boston at 3 A.M. on Monday morning, we were exhausted. That evening, Sandra showed up with a team of guys from her church. They had rented a full-size cargo van, brought pizzas for the kids, and took me to the grocery store to buy goodies from America for our return trip to China. I will always remember Sandra Suzio and those kind Baptist men as angels sent by God to help us in our hour of need.

By the time we returned to China, we had witnessed so many "miracles," I lost count of them all. First, John and Dinah Watkins helped us get in touch with the consul general, who got us visas and opened the door for us to leave. Without the generosity of United Airlines, Norman Kaplan, Ron Martin, and Holiday Inn Select, we could not have afforded to fly to and stay in Boston. And, we never could have made it to the hospital to release Levi and then get to the airport on time without Sandra Suzio's help. And if I hadn't met Kay Warren for 10 minutes in California six months prior, Sandra Suzio never would have learned about Levi. Like discovering second cousins twice removed, people were connecting through Levi in the most improbable ways. The world was starting to seem like one great big chain of love melded together by a single orphan.

CHAPTER NINE

Light in Me

Didn't you say you wanted to find Me?
Well here I am. There you are. So what now?
—STEVEN CURTIS CHAPMAN FROM "WHAT NOW?"

救

WE HAD BARELY UNPACKED OUR bags and settled back into life in China when the SARS epidemic broke out. Sudden Acute Respiratory Syndrome washed over East Asia, leaving a wake of fear and death behind. Beijing was the epicenter of the disease with nearly half the world's cases originating from the city. Beijing residents, both Chinese and foreigners, donned surgical masks to try to keep from catching and spreading the disease. Tollbooth workers even wore hazardous material suits to protect themselves from head to toe. As daily reports of casualties splashed across the headlines, our families back in America became increasingly fearful for our safety. At the same time, Levi had experienced a marked growth spurt and his wounds were again splitting open. This meant he needed more surgery—and fast!

Our friend Kimberly Fitzgerald, who owned a beautiful house in California, offered us plane tickets to America and a safe haven from SARS at her home for as long as we needed. We were also able to connect with Dr. David Greenhalgh from Shiners Hospitals for Children–Northern California, who offered to pick up on Levi's surgery where Dr. Schulz, Dr. Sheridan, and their Boston team had left off. With so many people from the orphanage making an exodus back to the States, John volunteered to stay in Langfang to continue running the orphanage and stay with Miao Miao. Since she was a Chinese citizen, we could not take her out of China with us.

Miao Miao had endured two failed adoptions by this point. Day by day, we watched her emotionally withdraw as despair set in. She was exhibiting classic symptoms of Attachment Disorder. Attachment Disorder is a common phenomenon among orphans who live in institutions. It occurs during the first few years of life when a child doesn't have a parental figure in his or her life with whom he or she can bond. This basic loss results in ongoing feelings of rage, deep shame, a lack of trust, and a fear of attaching to anyone. We had never heard of this disorder when we lived in the States. All I knew about it was what I could see in Miao Miao.

One day I got an e-mail from my friends Jeff and Wanda Jeffers who had adopted a child from Asia and were aware of this issue. They listed 16 signs of Attachment Disorder. Miao Miao had 11 of them. Though she had been matched with a new family in the States, we watched and waited with trepidation. *What if this one falls through too?* we wondered. *What will become of Miao Miao?*

With each failed adoption, John and I wondered anew if it was God's will for us to become her forever family. We always stopped short of making the decision, though, because she would again get matched to a new family and she would begin to imagine being with them. We knew that Levi would need lifelong physical care, and we feared we might be overtaxing our entire family if we adopted Miao Miao as well.

Why does God allow this girl to keep being rejected? John and I wondered. There was a good family from Tennessee who wanted to adopt Miao Miao and had been working on her adoption for over a year. As they entered the final stage of the adoption process and were requesting to be matched to Miao Miao, we prayed fervently that God would honor that request. Unfortunately, that day never arrived. The China Center for Adoption Affairs (CCAA) disapproved the adoption because the Tennessee family was trying to adopt Miao Miao outside the parameters of the system. They gave the family another child instead. But the result was that Miao Miao's heart was broken again.

We were all devastated and wondered why God had said no to our prayers. Once again, Miao Miao had to be told that the family whose picture hung on her bed would not be coming after all. The sad duty fell to her foster parent, Mike Haller. "Don't lose heart," he tried to console her. "God will give you a family."

"I don't believe God," Miao Miao quietly answered. Her

words broke our hearts. She had decided God—not to mention people—could not be trusted.

Shortly after this third failed adoption, the Christian musician Steven Curtis Chapman and his wife, Mary Beth, came to the children's village to adopt one of our babies, little Maria. Typically, when visitors arrive at the orphanage, all the older children swarm them. On this particular day, while all the other kids gathered around Steven to hear him play his guitar and sing, Miao Miao stood in the corner by herself. This was highly unusual, but it signaled her despair.

Steven noticed her out of the corner of his eye. Moved by her obvious despair, he was inspired to write the song "What Now?" for his *All Things New* album. He dedicated the song to her and the first two lines of the song are hers: "I saw the face of Jesus/In a little orphan girl." Later Steven told us that it was their experience meeting Miao Miao that was part of their inspiration for starting Shaohannah's Hope, a foundation that assists adoptive families.

Miao Miao's desperate need for a family reignited the question for John and me: Should we adopt Miao Miao? Was God reserving us as her forever family? Would we be able to manage adopting both Levi and Miao Miao?

John brought to God his list of reasons why adopting Miao Miao wasn't a good idea: We had too many kids; this may spread our love too thin; home-schooling is already a challenge; we don't have the money. Then John opened his Bible to 1 John 4 and read:

And so we know and rely on the love God has for us.
God is love. Whoever lives in love lives in God, and God
in him. In this way, love is made complete among us so
that we will have confidence on the day of judgment,
because in this world we are like him. There is no fear in
love. But perfect love drives out fear. (verses 16-18)

John had tears running down his face as he read these
words. After he told me about his experience, we both knew
we could rely on God to take care of the practical concerns
with adopting Miao Miao.

We brought her into our home to live before officially
beginning the adoption process. We also renamed her Orly, a
Hebrew name that means "I have light in me." It was risky putting the cart before the horse. We knew the painful reality of
doing this from watching what happened to baby Grace, a
child who was to be adopted by one of my best friends, Kimberly Fitzgerald. Kimberly had crossed all the t's and dotted all
the i's on the adoption application and was simply waiting for
it to be finalized. Everything appeared to be moving smoothly
until one day a high-profile Chinese woman from Beijing came
to tour the orphanage at Langfang. We often had visitors and
gladly showed her around. What we didn't realize was that she
had more than a philanthropic interest in the orphans. She had
come to find a baby. Of all the babies in our orphanage, her
eyes settled on baby Grace.

"I'm sorry," I told the woman. "You are welcome to pick

any other child, but that little girl has already been matched with an adoptive mother." (The rules prohibiting preselection of a child for adoption do not apply to Chinese nationals.)

The Chinese woman refused to take no for an answer. At first we dug our heels in and remained unmoved by her forcefulness. Tension escalated when one of the owners of the compound that held our children's home got involved. Finally, in outrage he declared, "You have three days to move out!" In the last six months he had threatened to evict us from the foster homes three times over minor issues. We decided we were willing to risk getting kicked out for the sake of protecting my friend's pending adoption and asked him for additional time to find a new home for our orphans. He was stunned as he fully expected us to back down. After all, who would put their entire organization in jeopardy for the sake of one orphan?

Unfortunately, the landlord, not wanting to lose face in the eyes of the Chinese woman, came up with a new way to get baby Grace. He went over our heads to the Ministry of Civil Affairs, which finally gave us the order to release baby Grace to the woman. The message was clear: If we didn't turn over baby Grace to his friend, the government would shut down our entire organization.

It was one thing to be forced to relocate our foster home, but quite another to be put out of business. We lost the battle. The Chinese woman returned to retrieve Grace. I will never forget the moment when I picked up baby Grace from her baby bouncer and handed her over to her new mother. Grace had a new family and would be well taken care of. But my heart was broken for Kimberly who already considered Grace to be her daughter.

We took Orly in knowing we might have our hearts broken like this too. We might not be approved to adopt her— many things could go wrong. But her desperate need for a family superseded the potential grief we all might have to endure. With adoption proceedings underway for Levi also, we faced the same risk with him too. Now, however, the threat of SARS far outweighed any adoption problems we might encounter. We needed to escape from Beijing before it was too late. The government was growing desperate to control SARS and seemed ready to declare martial law if need be to prevent the spread of the disease. Beijing was about to be quarantined.

While I was worried for the whole family, Levi was my major concern. If he contracted SARS in his weakened state, would he survive?

John drove us all to the airport, intending to stay behind with just Orly. Levi still had time remaining on a previous medical visa, so getting him out of China was not an issue.

Just as we approached Beijing, my oldest son, Ian, then seven years old, announced he didn't feel well. Sure enough, he felt feverish. The government had mandatory temperature sensors set up throughout the airport to pinpoint individuals who might be carrying the SARS virus. If Ian was suspected of having SARS, he would be whisked away to a hospital. His U.S. citizenship did not protect him from these measures. These were facilities to quarantine anyone with a fever or any other symptom of SARS. Unfortunately, if you didn't have SARS going into the building, you might contract it while staying there. Too many people were dying at these hospitals.

When we arrived at the airport, we made the decision that it was too dangerous to take Ian through the airport screening. Although this was the prudent course, I was not emotionally prepared for this. Ian was supposed to be coming with me to California and getting out of harm's way. I felt like my son was being ripped away from me.

Almost before I even realized what was happening, I was waving good-bye to John and Ian as the van pulled away. I had no idea when I would see them again.

We went to Kimberly's house in Dixon, California. During this time we were able to get Levi checked in at Shriners Hospitals for Children–Northern California, where he received another round of much-needed skin grafts. Unfortunately, not all skin grafts go smoothly. His skin itched so badly he ended up scratching the entire new patch of skin off during the night. We awoke to a bloody mess and faced yet another surgery the next day to correct this mishap. We spent two months shuttling between Shriners and Kimberly's house. The severe measures implemented by the Chinese government were successful and the SARS quarantine was lifted. John and Ian were able to meet up with us in California while Orly stayed behind in the care of other teammates. We had been separated for one month.

Finally, after spending an unexpected summer in the States, we all made our way back to China where some surprising developments awaited. I had gone to California feeling like our lives had been put on hold. In reality, we were merely making a pit stop to prepare us to get back into the race that lay ahead.

救

Doors seemed to fly open for us to complete Orly's adoption once we made the decision to bring her into our family. We were able to raise the money we needed to cover her adoption expenses, which was fortunate because we were flat broke. Steven and Mary Beth Chapman generously helped us through Shaohannah's Hope Foundation. Our unexpected trip overseas had wiped us out financially. Now with six kids in our home, we were beginning to feel the budget strain of extra mouths to feed and clothes to buy, not to mention the physical and emotional wear and tear they took on us. Even so, John and I moved forward, confident we had made the right decision about Orly and Levi.

We soon discovered this decision didn't meet with everyone's approval. To complete our adoption dossier, I needed to provide my birth certificate. I needed a new copy, and privacy laws in California prohibit anyone except for immediate family members to obtain one. My dad lives in Hollywood Hills. When we contacted him to request his help in obtaining the document, he demurred.

The plans for Orly came to a grinding halt. Without this document, her adoption could be delayed indefinitely. "Lord, we need to find a way to motivate my dad to cooperate with us," John and I prayed. Soon after, a big tour bus pulled up outside the orphanage with approximately 60 passengers. Out walked six-foot, seven-inch Anthony Robbins, one of the world's most famous motivational speakers. He is the CEO of several major companies and has counseled people like Nelson Mandela, Mikhail Gorbachev, and Tony Blair.

As the group crowded into one of our children's homes, John stepped up on a stool and began telling them about our lives and our faith. Tony Robbins, so moved by John's words, came up to him, kissed him on his head, and said, "I just want you to know, you're beautiful people." John then took the group over to the orphanage.

Whenever visitors come, John can hold their attention until the orphans come out. Then the visitors get distracted by the kids because they're so cute. Oddly, though, Tony Robbins continued to listen to John, who was sharing about how we had been walking by faith since coming to China.

"John, can you give us some examples of what you mean by that?" Tony interrupted. When John started giving specific examples from our lives, all of Tony's platinum partners—highly successful businesspeople throughout the United States—began to set down the kids and crowd around John, hanging on his every word. At the end of John's talk, the visitors started playing with the orphans again. One little girl got

Tony Robbins's attention. Of the 80 kids who were now in our care, he zeroed in on one brightly shining light—Orly. He walked over to where she was playing. He picked her up and raised her toward the ceiling and in his signature motivational way said, "What can you *not* do? Nothing!" Orly giggled and played along. Tony fell in love with her. When he learned we were trying to adopt her, he asked John how our plans for her were going.

"It's going all right, except for a little snag we just hit." He explained to Tony how we needed my birth certificate to complete the adoption dossier, and because my dad was unwilling to do this for us, the adoption process would be delayed indefinitely.

When Tony asked John why my dad wasn't willing to help us, John said, "Lisa's dad is a logical man. We've got four of our own kids already, and now we're contemplating adopting two more. He thinks it's too much. Her dad loves her very much, and he doesn't want Lisa to have a hard life by getting in over her head with too many children. He just doesn't understand how we live by faith and trust that this decision is the right one. He needs some motivation."

Tony answered, "John, the life you guys are living is the life more people should live. This is the ideal way. Where does your father-in-law live?"

John told Tony that my dad lived in Hollywood Hills.

"My headquarters are in San Diego," Tony said. "When I get back to California, I'll go talk to your father-in-law."

John thanked him, but as they drifted apart and John started talking to other people from Tony's organization, they said, "You don't realize what just happened, do you?"

John said, "Yeah, Tony said he was going to help."

"No, you're not getting it," they continued. "Tony Robbins is the world's foremost motivational speaker, and he just said he was going to call your father-in-law and motivate him. He doesn't stand a snowball's chance . . ."

The snow had started to fall by the time the platinum member club was ready to load their tour bus again. As we stood outside in the softly falling whiteness, waving good-bye to our visitors, it felt as if we were being anointed with the cool oil of comfort and grace.

As it turned out, my dad caught wind that Tony Robbins was planning to drop in for a visit to "motivate" him, and he ended up sending my birth certificate before Tony could ever come knocking!

CHAPTER TEN

A Child Shall Lead Them

If your vision is for a year,
plant wheat.
If your vision if for 10 years,
plant trees.
If your vision is for a lifetime,
plant people.
—CHINESE PROVERB

救

ORLY'S ADOPTION PROCESS TOOK center stage the following year. Levi had been with our family for as long as he could remember, so he had no concept of adoption. To him, we had always been Mommy and Daddy. Orly, on the other hand, had watched baby after baby parade out of the orphanage ahead of her to be with their forever families. At first she wondered when her turn would come, but later she gave up hope that it would ever come.

After overcoming the hurdle of getting my birth certificate from my father, we felt like the road had been paved for Orly's adoption to become final. Of course, I knew not to get too far ahead of myself on these things. Her adoption could be thwarted in a million different ways.

When Orly came to live with us, it was a big shock for her. Though the walk from the foster home to our house was just one block, it might as well have been around the world in terms of culture. Orly went from hearing Chinese spoken by the nannies all day to hearing English spoken by two adults and four other children. She knew how to speak some English, but for several weeks after she came to our house, she barely even made a sound, and she he was scared to death of our dog, Wilson.

Gradually she began to trust that her sojourn into our home was not just for a visit; it would be for a lifetime. Some of the troubling Attachment Disorder symptoms we had been concerned about began to diminish. Bit by bit, our rough-and-tumble household looked less threatening and more inviting to Orly. Eventually she started opening up to us. Her quiet, gentle demeanor brought a welcome balance to the constant frenzy of three young boys, and Emily finally got the little sister she had always hoped for. Watching Orly's transformation after joining our family affirmed that we had made the right decision.

Nonetheless, we continued to hold our breath, knowing that with adoption, "it ain't over till it's over." While we waited, several unexpected visitors came knocking at our foster home door. One day a truckload of soldiers arrived at our doorstep.

These soldiers turned out to be military doctors who had come on a goodwill mission. Along with delivering much-needed medical supplies, they performed physical exams on the children. We had received so many orphans who required surgeries, and on our overstretched budget, we simply did not know where the resources would come from to meet these needs.

These soldiers were like streams of water in the desert for us. The senior doctor, a full colonel, had an entire hospital, dental clinic, and scores of doctors, nurses, dentists, and surgeons at his disposal. Having heard of our work, he brought his senior staff to see firsthand. They were touched by what they saw and offered to provide surgeries and dental treatment for the children for free or at a greatly reduced cost. The colonel told us that our example as foreigners coming all the way to China to help their orphans had challenged them to do more for China's orphans.

Their response to the orphans was very different from the initial response of our 60-something-year-old staff doctor: "Why do you keep bringing these broken children in?" she asked. "Can't you bring some healthy ones? Don't you know how hard it is to keep these kids alive?"

We told her, "That's the point. If we don't care for these children, who will?" This was the beginning of a transformation in her heart and spiritual outlook. Not long after that, when Ann Lo was talking with her about Jesus, she decided to become a Christian.

The media attention Levi had received during his first journey to Boston sparked international interest and eventually spread from China to the United States and to places as far away as Great Britain. Beijing is the capital of China, and as such, many of the foreigners living there are diplomats. Over time they heard about our work. For instance, Avenal McKinnon, the wife of New Zealand's Ambassador to China, sponsored a fashion show in Beijing to benefit several charities, including our orphanage. This exposure brought us much-needed funding and support from new sources previously unacquainted with us. On another occasion, we experienced what John called "a British invasion" when one day a Jaguar pulled into our compound with the union jack flying on the front fender. Our three guests were the Lady Carole Blackshaw, the Lady Mayoress of the City of London; the wife of the British Ambassador to China; and the wife of the Sheriff of Nottingham.

On first impression, Lady Blackshaw appeared to fit the stereotype of a stiff-upper-lipped Briton. Boy, was I wrong. As she toured our children's homes, she began to be visibly moved by what she was seeing—especially when she saw Levi. Patting her teary eyes dry, she rejoined the group for pictures and proceeded to scoop Levi into her arms to give him a tight squeeze. After returning to London, she called me directly to check on his progress and to offer to assist us if we ever needed surgeries for him in Great Britain.

Our big media break came when *Morning Edition* with Bob Edwards covered a story about seven special-needs babies from the Jiaozuo orphanage in Henan province who came to our orphanage in Langfang.

The audience for this program in America is estimated to

be 16 million, not including listeners in other countries. On the day when millions of Americans were expecting to hear a story recapping 9/11 and the war on terror that followed, they instead heard a story about special-needs babies being helped in China.

John didn't think too much about this statistic during the interview, but when he saw his e-mail in-box in the days following the interview, he was stunned by the magnitude of the response. He received a tidal wave of e-mails from around the world. The majority came from the States, but others came from Japan, Australia, and even Iraq. He and Tim spent days struggling to keep up with the flood of e-mails coming in. Many people e-mailed to say that they were moved to tears as they listened to the broadcast. Others admitted that while they were not Christians, they nonetheless thanked God that people like us existed. That month fifty thousand people visited our Web site and had the opportunity to read about Levi and our work with orphans. The people's compassion poured forth in an unprecedented increase in financial support for our foster homes. More than 400 people requested to be added to our mailing list.

We thought things would begin to settle down after a week or so, but instead life went from wild to surreal. We received an e-mail from CBS saying that *60 Minutes II* also wanted to do a story on the orphanage. Apparently President Bush's cabinet members tuned in to *Morning Edition* that day also, because not long after, we received a call from the U.S. Embassy in Beijing telling us that Tommy Thompson, then Health and

Human Services Secretary, wanted to come to China to meet our team and tour our foster-children facilities.

Not long after, U.S. Labor Secretary Elaine Chao was scheduled to come to Beijing for some high-level meetings. When Secretary Thompson heard she was coming to Beijing, he told her not to leave without paying a visit to the children's village in Langfang. She entered our compound in a black Lincoln with the U.S. flag flying on the front corner. She was accompanied by a long motorcade with her own security detail, plus Chinese police vehicles and lights flashing. Unfortunately, she didn't leave the orphanage as dignified and immaculately dressed as she had arrived. She had given the children candy for a treat, and one child smeared his chocolate-covered hands all over her pastel sweater when they hugged good-bye. Despite the mess, she enjoyed meeting the children, and we felt privileged to be visited and encouraged by such high-ranking U.S. officials.

救

There's a saying in China: "It's not good for a man to get too famous or for a pig to get too fat." We had learned this all too well the day the Chinese lady from the prominent family walked in and saw baby Grace. As devastating as it was for Kimberly to lose baby Grace, this event lit a fire under us to find a new location for a foster home. Our landlord had threatened to evict us too many times, and we knew we could not build our work on such a shaky foundation. We needed to find land of our own to build a new foster home.

Our dream was to create a brand-new children's village designed from the ground up to meet our orphans' needs. After running the orphanage for three years, we had a good idea of the environment and equipment that were needed to provide full-service care. Although we investigated several different areas, the price was always the same: U.S.$220,000 for approximately six acres of land.

The day came when we needed to make a decision to buy. Again, with no apparent source of provision, we planned to select one of the available parcels and move forward in faith that God would provide for us. We narrowed down our search to three pieces of land. The problem was that John favored one and Tim favored another.

When the day arrived where we had to make a decision, they prayed and asked God to choose which portion of land He wanted us to have and to make it clear to both of them so that there would be no doubt in either of their minds. About a half hour after praying that prayer, they received a surprise visit at the orphanage from both the mayor and the vice-mayor about a parcel of land that neither Tim nor John favored. The dignitaries had come in person to find out about the decision.

The mayor indicated that he wanted to talk to us about it, and so they invited him to our house. Mark Wei was called in as an interpreter. When the mayor asked what was complicating the decision, the men told him that each parcel had pros and cons. The mayor emphatically said that he wanted to establish a foster home in his jurisdiction, so he asked John and Tim to name their price.

They knew this was an opportunity to lowball him in the Chinese tradition of bartering. As they were discussing this and before they could even answer, the mayor cut in and announced that he would sell all 25 mu (six acres) for one Chinese dollar (approximately 12 cents).

Because John was still learning Chinese, he wasn't sure he had heard the mayor properly and so he asked Mark, "Did I hear that wrong? It sounded like he said one dollar."

"No," Mark replied, "you heard him right. He said 'One dollar!'"

We named the site of our future foster homes Grace Children's Village after the baby who set this turn of events in motion.

And as for wondering where the money would come from to pay for our new children's village, Levi's story provided yet another unexpected influx of support. Life Outreach International, a Christian television program in the States, flew to China with a camera crew and produced a moving six-minute video of Levi's story. When they aired this segment on one of their daily shows, we received over $200,000, enough seed money to get the construction started on Grace Children's Village. Not long after, Adam and Karen Robarts, owners of Robarts Interiors, one of Beijing's premier architectural design firms, agreed to donate their expertise on this project to fulfill their own dream of one day designing a village for orphans. Many of the additional building supplies, from the concrete to the roof tiles, were donated by local and international companies. Who would have guessed one abandoned baby would produce such a harvest of generosity?

As we waited anxiously to finalize Orly's adoption, we wondered at the irony: *Will Levi, one of China's most famous orphans, ever end up getting adopted?*

CHAPTER ELEVEN

Putting Things Right

Everything that could be shaken was shaken
And all that remains is all I ever really had.
—RICH MULLINS, FROM "HOME"

ONE OF ORLY'S FAVORITE books is P. D. Eastman's *Are You My Mother?* The first time I read it to her, she looked up at me with a big, knowing smile. The story is about a bird that hatches only to find itself alone in the nest. Unbeknownst to the baby bird, its mother had flown away to find it a worm. Confused and alone, the rest of the story recounts how the baby bird searches for its mother. Orly was on the same search. Time and again, she thought she'd found her "mother" only to be disappointed.

Finally, on Thanksgiving Day 2004, Orly triumphantly walked through our front door, adoption papers in hand. She was officially a Bentley! No longer would she wonder who she belonged to or what her mother looked like. We all breathed a big sigh of relief as we feasted on turkey and all the trimmings, American style. We had much to be grateful for that day. One adoption down, one to go.

Now, the question remained: Could we pull this off again with Levi? In China, it's all about the *guanxi,* or relationship. It's about who you know and how well you are connected. I may not speak much Mandarin, but *guanxi* was a language I became fluent in. My encounter with the doctor in the Langfang hospital when I tried to have Levi released to the Beijing Children's Hospital taught me my first lesson in *guanxi.* I couldn't use my American pushiness to get what I wanted. It took Mr. Sun's *guanxi* with the hospital to get Levi transferred to Beijing. Likewise, it was Mark Wei's *guanxi* with Chinese officials that opened the way for us to get Levi documented and on his overseas flight-for-life in record time. It would take mega-*guanxi* to adopt Levi.

The first and most formidable hurdle to jump was getting our file "matched" to Levi's. This was no small feat. One impediment was that we were trying to get prematched to Levi in contravention of the rules set by the China Center for Adoption Affairs. Normally, when an orphan is funneled into the adoption process, his or her file is sent from the originating orphanage to the CCAA. The CCAA carefully determines which adoption agency would be the best match for each orphan. In our case, we needed to be sure that Levi's file was sent to Children's Hope International, the adoption agency we were using. Every orphan's file includes a picture of the child, and on Levi's, there was a photograph of him as a burned infant. Whoever reviewed his file at the CCAA thought that his injuries were too severe and determined him to be ineligible for international adoption.

The second impediment was that CCAA's guidelines for adoption limit the number of children in a family to a maximum of five. Levi would be number six for us! If ever we needed John's legal expertise, it was now. He set to work drafting letters to Chinese authorities, requesting an exemption from the five-child regulation, explaining our unique ability to help Levi due to our connections with Shriners Hospitals, our experience working with special-needs children, etc. Things on earth may have been stacked against us, but we didn't despair—we prayed. The only *guanxi* that would help us now would be heaven's.

救

It was one week before Christmas. Just Levi and I were home, so the house was unusually quiet. Levi was sitting on the living room rug, the floor lamp casting its light on him like a spotlight. With an audience of one, he stood up shakily and took his first step. Wobbly though it was, one step became two, then three, until he had made his way across the room. I clapped and shouted with excitement. *Levi can walk! The doctors were wrong—we won't have to amputate his foot!* Nothing compared to this Christmas gift that year. In the months that followed, Levi mastered walking, then running, jumping, skip-ping—all the things a little boy does.

His newfound mobility came to an abrupt stop just after the New Year. The skin on his left leg had ruptured and was bleeding. It was time for his next "cut and release" surgery. United Airlines was again willing to provide airfare to the States, and Shriners Hospitals for Children–Los Angeles agreed to see Levi, but not until March. We waited for the appointed time, but when we got to L.A., the doctors said, "Yes, he needs surgery, but we can't schedule you for three more months." They had no openings on their surgical calen-dar. Crestfallen, I tried to explain. "We live in China," I said. "We can't afford to go back and then return here in three months, and I can't stay in the States for three months to wait, nor do I want to be apart from my family that long." They had no solution for us.

I left the hospital room defeated. *God, what am I going to do? We came all this way for nothing and Levi's wounds are get-ting worse.* I walked around the corner and saw a pay phone. *Maybe there's one person who can help me,* I thought. I stepped inside and dialed Dr. Greenhalgh at Shriners Hospitals for Children–Northern California. He had done Levi's last round of skin grafts; maybe he could help again. When I explained what had happened in Los Angeles, Dr. Greenhalgh told me to get a car and drive to Sacramento. He would get Levi in for sur-gery immediately.

The next morning, which was Saturday, Emily, Ian, Levi,

and I loaded in the car and made our way north through California. We met with Dr. Greenhalgh first thing on Monday morning and he scheduled Levi for a Wednesday surgery. Over the next few days, doctors at Shriners performed the necessary surgeries on Levi. Afterward, the nurses gave me intensive training on how to care for his wounds and change his bandages. I nearly passed out the first time I had to do it myself. The wounds are always the worst immediately after a surgery.

Dr. Greenhalgh's spontaneous response to my call for help was another link in the chain of compassion that was being forged for Levi.

救

With trips once—sometimes twice—each year to the United States for Levi's medical needs, the cost to care for him was beyond our means, especially considering the fact that we had no medical insurance to help defray the expenses. Also, the cost of an international adoption is over U.S.$15,000. We might be able to slip in through the back door to be matched to Levi, but there would be no "back door" to avoid paying for his adoption. Fortunately, Children's Hope International, the adoption agency that had so generously paid for Levi's initial surgeries in China, gave us a generous grant. Melody Zhang, who ran the Beijing office of CHI is one of my closest friends. I consider her to be my Chinese sister. Melody knew that we were Levi's best hope for a great life. Shaohannah's Hope also helped fill in the financial gap. So now, with money no longer an obstacle to adopting Levi, we still had the issue of getting matched to him.

It didn't take long to get back into the game in China. John and I were roaring full-speed ahead, rpms constantly pushing the red line. The Bakers had returned to California for a year on furlough, which left John busy running the ministry. My days were filled with meetings in Beijing, speaking engagements, public relations, implementing nurture training with our nannies, and reviewing our medical program for the 90 orphans in our care. Nannies cared for our own children while we cared for all of the other kids and ran the ministry. We didn't see what was wrong with this picture for a long time. Every now and then we'd catch glimpses of ourselves in the rearview mirror, so to speak, and realize we were maybe driving a little too fast. But there was no time to slow down. Babies were dying. They needed our help.

John and I rarely spent time alone anymore. Our relationship had become more of a business partnership. We would share stories about progress we each were making on different fronts, and we prayed for each other, but it wasn't like we were approaching our work as one. Our adventure in China wasn't creating intimacy between us. In fact, in the few years we had lived in China, we had erected a great wall of our own, brick by brick—one that was threatening to divide us. Recognizing that our marriage was in trouble and our family was out of whack, I turned to my life coach, Allen Tappe, for counsel.

I met Allen in 1986 during my first year of college at Abilene Christian University in Texas. The very first week of school I almost got kicked out for drinking on campus. I was given two choices—go to Allen for counseling or be sent back to Hollywood. Allen must have scratched his head the first time I walked into his office with my wild hair, turquoise jeans, and red mohair boots. But far from judging me, Allen accepted me. I eventually came to know his wife, Barbara, and they both treated me like a daughter.

救

Raising six kids is hard work. Raising six kids while maintaining a growing ministry and caring for 90-plus orphans and managing all the details that go with it can be downright exhausting. Not surprisingly, John and I had become victims of battle fatigue. But on Allen's recommendation, we decided to return to the States for a year of furlough.

No surprise, we chose to go to Arlington, Texas, which was where Allen and Barbara live. For the first time, we were able to bring both Orly and Levi, too. We got permission to bring Levi with us so he could receive more surgery. Though neither John nor I was from Texas, we knew Allen would help walk us through the long, dark tunnel that lay before us. Over time and through extensive, wise counsel, John and I began to sort out what had gone wrong for us in China. Our priorities had gotten mixed-up and off-kilter. It was humbling to have to leave the field in China we were two broken people who knew we had to realign our lives and get ourselves back on track.

A quote from Corrie ten Boom sums up my feelings about China at the time: "I've learned to hold everything with an open hand, because if God has to pry it away, it will hurt." John and I both felt God pulling our hands off of China and all we had built there. Just a month earlier I had been in China telling a group of visitors that they could "bury my boots here." China was our home and the only place I wanted to be. As John and I addressed our individual issues that were creating problems in our marriage, we were able to gradually break down our great wall and rebuild something beautiful. Shortly into our furlough, we started sensing that God had shut the door behind us at the children's village at Langfang. John and I both wanted to return to China, but we knew it would be under a new set of circumstances.

Texas was our crucible—the fire chamber where God refined our characters. It also became the place where we felt the intense heat of Levi's adoption process. On a December morning, the phone rang. I picked it up and was surprised to hear a voice from China: Melody Zhang was on the other end of the line. Even more startling was her news: She had gone to CCAA and personally asked them to allow Levi's file to go to her adoption agency. She gave CCAA a personal guarantee that this baby would be adopted to the family best able to care for his ongoing medical needs. Melody put her *guanxi* on the line for us. She used her job, and excellent reputation, to save Levi from becoming a lifelong orphan. The CCAA agreed to place his file with her agency, which was a tremendous first-round win. But it was no guarantee of victory.

Now, with his file moving from the CCAA to Melody's office at CHI, we needed to be sure everything in our file was accurate and current. Specific legal requirements such as fingerprints and signed documents expire after a certain point. If anything in our dossier had expired by the time it got to CHI, our chance to be matched with Levi again would disappear.

When Melody finally received Levi's file at CHI, she once more had to call up special favors to make sure our file was actually matched to Levi's. Successful at this point, round two went to the Bentleys!

What happened next felt like a knockout, and I didn't even see it coming.

After Melody matched our file with Levi's, she had to send it back to the CCAA for final approval. When Levi's file streamed back through the CCAA, the agent handling it noticed his picture on the file. Days later we received a letter in Texas with this message: "We're sorry, but this baby is not available for adoption. He is too badly burned and we do not feel you would be able to take proper care of him."

We were devastated. *Oh no!* We reeled at the news. *How were we going to straighten this out?* For all of Melody's hard work, lines still got crossed in the end. The CCAA didn't realize that we already knew about Levi's needs and were still willing to adopt him. My mind started racing ahead. *What if we lose Levi?* Ian, Oliver, and Donald "Reid" are brothers to him. They pull him across the room, roughhouse, and roll around like a bunch of puppies. Emily and Orly would miss their baby brother with all their hearts. *God,* I begged in prayer, *don't let us lose him now!*

With nowhere else to turn, I called Melody, and she agreed to go to bat for us one more time. This would be her last chance to save Levi. Risking being labeled a troublemaker and losing *guanxi,* Melody went before the CCAA and presented a case for why we, the Bentleys, should be able to adopt Levi. The CCAA wanted proof that we would be able to care for him—that we understood the magnitude of his burns and the ongoing treatment he would require. It was reassuring to know how concerned China was for its orphans. And yet, I wondered at the irony: To think that after all we had gone through to help save this little boy, we now have to prove ourselves worthy of adopting him.

While we waited for an outcome, Levi continued running, jumping, and playing without a clue that the outcome of his future family hung in the balance.

救

Veiled from any knowledge of what was transpiring in China, we prayed diligently for Melody's success in helping us adopt Levi. As we awaited an answer, Texas brought us some God-sized opportunities. On a rare visit to the U.S., Ye Xiaowen, China's Director of The State Administration of Religious Affairs, invited John to meet with him at the Chinese consulate in Houston. Ye Xiaowen is a member of the Chinese cabinet and the official that makes religious policy in China, so he's a hugely important figure in the Chinese government. John's dream had been to build bridges between America's Christian community and China's communist government. This meeting was an important step in that direction. From that meeting, Secretary Ye invited John and a delegation of evangelical Christian leaders to China for an unprecedented meeting with senior members of the Chinese government. John hoped to demonstrate the positive effect Christianity has on any society that embraces its principles. The work we had done on behalf of orphans was a practical example of good. Along with this breakthrough delegation, John was also invited to Washington, D.C., to meet China's Ambassador to the United States, Zhou Wenzhong. We felt as if God was saying, "If you can't be in China, then I'll bring China to you." These unexpected meetings with high-level Chinese officials served as a great affirmation to continue the work we had begun.

John and I also were invited to speak at many churches and schools while we were on furlough. One of these speaking engagements had significant meaning to me. Abilene Christian University invited me to return and speak to its student body, which was ironic because 20 years earlier I had nearly been kicked out of that college for drinking. I was overwhelmed by the positive reception I received by the students and faculty at ACU.

At each place we visited during our yearlong furlough we had the chance to tell Levi's story and how his little life had affected so many others, including our own, and how our work saving orphans continued to provide a gateway into areas

of world influence. By this time, the chain of people attached
to Levi's life could have stretched around the world.

救

Scar tissue does not grow. For Levi this means every year
until he is an adult, he will need to undergo "cut and release"
surgery to prevent his growth from being stunted. While we
were in Texas, his skin started to open up again. I tried to prepare Levi for what the doctors would do, and I warned him
it would hurt afterward. Before he drifted into an anesthesia-
induced sleep, Levi said, "I'm a big boy now. I'm not gonna
cry." The medical staff in the room marveled at his resolve.

John and I came to Texas needing some "cut and release"
surgery of our own. Our relationship had calloused, and scar
tissue was keeping us from growing any further. Though it was
painful and uncomfortable, healing eventually came.

We returned to China exactly one year to the day I had left.
Armed with a new vision for how to serve special-needs
orphans, we launched Harmony Outreach and are planting
orphanages in the unreached regions of inland China where the
needs are the greatest. This goal was combined with a plan to
develop ways to bridge relations between America and China.
Like walking into a fog, we weren't entirely sure where this path
would end. And yet we continued to move forward, trusting that
God had gone ahead of us to clear the way. Harmony seemed
like an appropriate image for us too. John and I had worked

hard to bring our individual lives, our family, our marriage, and our work into balance—to put things right.

救

In September 2006, John took Levi with him to Guangzhou, the city where all orphans and their new parents go to finalize their adoptions. On the day Levi officially become a Bentley, he was as proud as Orly had been when she walked into the house holding her adoption papers. It had been a long journey from the field to our front door. For him, though, the paperwork was all just details. He felt he had always been one of us. The last legal step in this adoption process will be landing him on American soil to obtain his U.S. citizenship.

Levi's story is unfinished. If I could and it were up to me, I would take away all of his wounds and give him back all that the burns took from him. I would in a heartbeat. But you know, one day Levi will tell his story his way. And it may not, probably will not, line up with mine. Maybe he will say, "No Mom, all these hardships have made me who I am." I am just a link in a chain that has connected the hearts of people around the world. Levi may have been left in a field to die, but through God's providence, this boy was destined to live.

Epilogue

*You were shown these things so that you might know
that the LORD is God; besides him there is no other.*

—DEUTERONOMY 4:35

ONE DAY I WAS DRIVING IN CHINA with all the kids in the car. I glanced in the rearview mirror and counted the number of heads—one, two, three, four, five, six. Stopping at Orly, I couldn't imagine what I would have missed out on if we hadn't brought her into our family. I wonder the same thing about Levi. What if Mr. Wang hadn't taken that first step of faith, and merely walked away like all the others? Instead he picked him up, and that began the story of saving Levi.

Jesus said that when He returns, He's going to separate us into two groups—those who saw the hurting—the ones in prison, the sick, the naked, the homeless—and helped, and those who kept on walking. Interestingly, the people God says we are to help are those who can never repay us—orphans, the elderly, and widows. They're vulnerable. When you give someone something without any expectation of getting anything in return, Jesus said, this is what I see and feel. In other words, whatever we do for the least of these, we're doing for Him. It's not our job to figure out if the parents were good or bad for abandoning their child. It is our job to see the need and help.

Our new foster home, Harmony Family House, is designed to take diamonds in the rough—even ones that are found in the dirt—and polish them up so that the world can see what treasures lay before it. We want to create a family environment instead of an institution to help our orphans attach with trust to the people around them. Instead of hiring nannies who merely work shifts and then go home, we hire Chinese house parents—a mom and a dad—so that the children gain a sense of stability. We want them to experience what it means to live in a family. We attempt to bring in children of different ages, so that the younger ones can learn from the older kids, and older ones learn how to care for and protect the younger ones.

After we went back, I decided to step down from my post as orphanage manager. John will lead this new venture while I manage our own home. We want to give the marriage foundation we laid in Texas time to set. As we nurture our vision for Harmony Family House, John will continue to pursue ways to dialogue with Chinese leaders. The *shu* might be an extinct character, but what it stands for is far from dead in China—or anywhere else in the world. Our goal is to let the *shu*—the spirit of unconditional love—live on.

The outreach part of our work will include going to the outer areas of China to help orphans no one else is helping— the essence of our new Keifeng project. We also want to come alongside impoverished Chinese families who decide to keep

their special-needs children but who cannot afford extra
expenses, such as hearing-aid batteries.

救

I have one of the baby booties Levi was wearing the day he was
found in the field. I've often wondered what his biological
mom was thinking when she dressed him in these booties and
his yellow burial outfit. She thought she was clothing him for
death. *Does she know he was saved?* Sometimes I wonder if she
has been peeking through the reeds all these years, like Moses'
mother when she was forced to abandon her son to the river
Nile. With all the media attention Levi has received throughout China, there's a good chance his family has been watching
us raise him at a distance. And who's to say this boy won't end
up in Pharaoh's household? Before he had even turned four,
Levi had held court before "kings" of the world—wise and
powerful leaders. Why would God choose this one life—and
an abandoned baby at that—to impact the world? It's the foolish confounding the wise.

I often think about that day in the field when Mr. Wang
saw Levi in his distress and decided to help, and I have no
words to describe my gratitude to him. What would have been
lost to the world if no one had believed Levi's life was like a
buried treasure?

As I run my hands over the dark, bumpy, thick skin on
Levi's back and legs, I know he will face a life of stares and
double takes, people wondering what in the world happened

to him. In one glance, many will walk away like the villagers in that field, never knowing the treasure they will be discarding.

I don't know that I would ever have enough energy for another Levi. But for now, for this one life, God gave me everything I needed to become his mother. In so many ways, I feel as if I'm sharing this role with everyone who had a hand in saving him. From Mr. Wang, to Mr. Sun, to Roberta Lipson, to Cynthia Qiu, to Nancy Fraser, to Dr. Schulz and Dr. Sheridan, to Linda and Don Evans—the list goes on and on. While John and I got the privilege of raising him, only one mother on this planet knows what it was like to bear Levi from her womb, to hear him cry for the first time, to feel him nurse contentedly at her breast. But countless numbers have borne him in their hearts.

About the Author

Lisa Misraje Bentley is an author and speaker. Lisa was born in Los Angeles to a Sephardic Jewish father and a Scandinavian Lutheran mother. Her parents' marriage didn't last long, and Lisa grew up trying to balance life between her mother's world in West Los Angeles and her father's world in the Hollywood Hills. Growing up she would say that she was half Jewish and half Christian. One day she realized that she could no longer be "half" of either, and at the age of 14 gave her heart to Jesus. But Lisa never lost her love for the Jewish people.

Lisa and her husband, John, are cofounders of Harmony Outreach (www.HarmonyOutreach.org), a ministry that operates a children's home for China's special-needs orphans and helps connect people and organizations to China. She has spoken all over North America and in China at churches, synagogues, business meetings, and conventions. She has been interviewed many times on radio, television, and for newspaper stories.

Lisa lives outside Beijing, China, with her husband, John, and their six children—two of whom are adopted from China. They have two pets: a cowardly dog named Wilson and an albino frog named Gary.

FOCUS ON THE FAMILY®

Welcome to the family!

Whether you purchased this book, borrowed it, or received it as a gift, we're glad you're reading it. It's just one of the many helpful, encouraging, and biblically based resources produced by Focus on the Family for people in all stages of life.

Focus began in 1977 with the vision of one man, Dr. James Dobson, a licensed psychologist and author of numerous best-selling books on marriage, parenting, and family. Alarmed by the societal, political, and economic pressures that were threatening the existence of the American family, Dr. Dobson founded Focus on the Family with one employee and a once-a-week radio broadcast aired on 36 stations.

Now an international organization reaching millions of people daily, Focus on the Family is dedicated to preserving values and strengthening and encouraging families through the life-changing message of Jesus Christ.

Focus on the Family Magazines

These faith-building, character-developing publications address the interests, issues, concerns, and challenges faced by every member of your family from preschool through the senior years.

| Focus on the Family **Citizen®** U.S. news issues | Focus on the Family **Clubhouse Jr.™** Ages 4 to 8 | Focus on the Family **Clubhouse™** Ages 8 to 12 | **Breakaway®** Teen guys | **Brio®** Teen girls 12 to 16 | **Brio & Beyond®** Teen girls 16 to 19 | **Plugged In®** Reviews movies, music, TV |

FOR MORE INFORMATION

Online:
Log on to www.family.org
In Canada, log on to www.focusonthefamily.ca

Phone:
Call toll free: (800) A-FAMILY (232-6459)
In Canada, call toll free: (800) 661-9800

More Great Resources
from Focus on the Family®

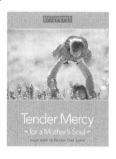

Tender Mercy for a Mother's Soul
Inspiration to Renew Your Spirit
By Angela Thomas
Written in the throes of motherhood, this book offers hope and inspiration. It will help renew moms' spirits by coming alongside them, recognizing their challenges, and guiding them toward deeper intimacy with God. Paperback

Wild Child, Waiting Mom
by Karilee Hayden and Wendi Hayden English
For 20 years, daughter Wendi left behind the values and love she had learned in her family and entered a downward spiral. During this time God brought Karilee the gift of hope that enabled her to pray for and love her daughter. An incredible story of God's redemption told by both mother and daughter. Paperback

Light from Lucas
by Bob Vander Plaats
The third of four children, Lucas was severely disabled at birth. Through the silent instruction of Lucas, the author and his family relates dozens of lessons they've learned—from knowing God and discovering the value of every life, to practical ideas on parenting and why we suffer. Paperback

FOR MORE INFORMATION

 Online:
Log on to www.family.org
In Canada, log on to www.focusonthefamily.ca.

 Phone:
Call toll free: (800) A-FAMILY
In Canada, call toll free: (800) 661-9800.

Focus
on the Family®

BP06XP1